International Cases in Sustainable Travel & Tourism

Edited by

Pierre Benckendorff
The University of Queensland

Dagmar Lund-Durlacher
MODUL University Vienna

(G) Goodfellow Publishers Ltd

 Published by Goodfellow Publishers Limited,
Woodeaton, Oxford, OX3 9TJ
http://www.goodfellowpublishers.com

British Library Cataloguing in Publication Data: a catalogue record for
this title is available from the British Library.

Library of Congress Catalog Card Number: on file.

ISBN: 978-1-908999-40-5

Copyright © Goodfellow Publishers Ltd 2013

 Design and typesetting by P.K. McBride, www.macbride.org.uk

Printed by Marston Book Services, www.marston.co.uk

Cover design by Cylinder, www.cylindermedia.com

Contents

Contributors

Christian Baumgartner studied landscape ecology and has been the Secretary General of Naturefriends International (www.nf-int.org) since 2005. Besides his work as lecturer for Sustainable Tourism in Vienna, Krems (A) and China, he is a member of the Tourism Sustainability Group within the EU Commission, DG enterprise and a member of several national and international tourism related advisory boards. Contact: christian.baumgartner@nf-int.org

Chris Briggs is the Director of Tourism and Recreation at the Great Barrier Reef Marine Park Authority in Townsville, Australia. Chris has over 12 years' experience in marine protected area management with experience both as a manager and in the field. He has an extensive background in marine tourism operations having worked and dived the length of the Great Barrier Reef over many years. Chris has been a key figure in establishing successful partnerships between the tourism industry and marine park managers to improve protection, presentation and stewardship of the Reef. Contact: chris.briggs@gbrmpa.gov.au

Michael Chiam Kah Min is a Senior Lecturer at the School of Business and Accountancy in Ngee Ann Polytechnic, Singapore. He teaches courses in tourism marketing, service quality in tourism and tourism research. His research interests include service quality, consumer behaviour, event management and sustainable tourism. Contact: michael_chiam@np.edu.sg

Paul Cunningham is a professor in the Department of Intercultural Communication at Rikkyo University, Japan. His research interests lie in the area of tourism, culture and communication, with a special interest in ecotourism, cultural and heritage tourism, sustainable development and environmental sociology. His primary research site is the Ogasawara Islands, located 1,000 kilometres south of Tokyo, where he has been exploring the cultural landscape and sense of place within the local community. Most recently, he has concluded an investigation of Cloughjordan Ecovillage in the Republic of Ireland in terms of the way in which this sustainable community governs itself. Contact: cunningh@rikkyo.ac.jp

Cynthia S. Deale is a professor in East Carolina University's School of Hospitality Leadership. She teaches a variety of hospitality and tourism courses and her research interests include the scholarship of teaching and learning, sustainability, and tourism and hospitality management practices. Dr Deale serves as a facilitator for the American Hotel & Lodging Association's Certified Hospitality Educator workshop and is a past president and board member of the International Council of Hotel, Restaurant and Institutional Education. She received her PhD from the University of Denver, her MSc from Michigan State University, and her BSc from the University of Puget Sound. Contact: ohalloranc@ecu.edu

Margaret Gooch is the Manager (Social and Economic Science) at the Great Barrier Reef Marine Park Authority in Townsville, Australia, where she is working with colleagues to develop and implement a social and economic long term monitoring program. Margaret's interests include education for sustainability, social resilience and the role of social science in natural resource management. She is particularly interested in the resilience of reef-dependent industries such as tourism and commercial fishing in the face of climate change. Margaret holds a PhD, BSc and Diploma of Teaching from Griffith University in Brisbane, and an MSc from James Cook University in Townsville. Contact: Margaret.Gooch@gbrmpa.gov.au

Nicole Häusler is a Partner and Senior Consultant of 'mascontour – Sustainable Tourism Consulting & Communication' located in Berlin. For more than fourteen years she has been focusing on Responsible Tourism Management and Training, the implementation of Corporate Social Responsibility (CSR) and Tourism & Poverty Reduction, especially in Asia and South America. She is also a member of the International Centre for Responsible Tourism (ICRT) in Leeds/Great Britain and a lecturer in the Master Programme of Sustainable Tourism Development at the University of Sustainable Development (FH) in Eberswalde near Berlin. Contact: haeusler@mascontour.info

Anja Hergesell is a research assistant at the University of Technology in Sydney and has worked as a researcher and lecturer at MODUL University Vienna. She is conducting her PhD studies on environmentally friendly tourist behaviour at the Vienna University of Economics and Business. Anja holds a Master's degree in European Tourism Management from Bournemouth University. She had worked as a research assistant at the University of Southern Denmark before starting her PhD studies. Anja has been involved with the BEST Education Network since 2003, serving first as secretary and later as an executive committee member. Her research interests include tourist behaviour and sustainable transport. Contact: anja_hergesell@yahoo.de

Dörte Kasüske holds an MSc in Tourism and Regional Planning – Management and Geography from Catholic University in Eichstaett Ingolstadt. She is the holder of a post-graduate scholarship of the Heinz-Nixdorf scholarship programme 2013, which aims to foster Asia-Pacific Experience (destination: India). She has international work experience in the Czech Republic, Myanmar and India. Contact: kasueske@mascontour.info

Brian E.M. King is professor and Associate Dean (Executive Education & Partnerships) in the School of Hotel & Tourism Management at Hong Kong Polytechnic University. He previously spent an extended period at Victoria University, Australia, in various roles including Head of School (Tourism and Hospitality) and Pro Vice-Chancellor. His PhD (Monash University) was on island resort tourism in Fiji and the Whitsundays and he has subsequently maintained a lasting research interest in island and resort tourism in Queensland. Contact brian.king@polyu.edu.hk

Dagmar Lund-Durlacher is Head of the Department of Tourism and Service Management and Dean of the Undergraduate School at MODUL University Vienna. She completed her doctoral studies at the Vienna University of Economics and Business. Prior to her appointment she directed a market research institute in Berlin and headed a Master Program for Sustainable Tourism Management at the University for Sustainable Development in Eberswalde (Germany). She is the acting chair of the BEST Education Network. Her current research interests focus on environmental management systems and eco certifications schemes for the tourism industry, green consumer behaviour, and corporate social responsibility. Contact: dagmar. lund-durlacher@modul.ac.at

Haretsebe A. Manwa is an Associate Professor at the North West University's Department of Tourism. She teaches a variety of tourism courses and her research interests include community-based tourism, tourism and poverty alleviation and heritage and cultural tourism. She has worked and researched widely in the Southern African Development Community member states (Botswana, Lesotho, South Africa and Zimbabwe). Dr Manwa has been instrumental in the restructuring of RETOSA, a regional tourism marketing organisation) she has also served on national/regional organisations e.g. Maloti Transfrontier Park Advisory Board (Lesotho), Quality Assurance Committee, and Biokavango Tourism Advisory Group (Botswana). Dr Manwa received her PhD from James Cook University, Australia. Contact: 23815310@nwu.ac.za or hmanwa@yahoo.com.au

Karmen Mentil has been a senior partner of the ÖAR Regionalberatung GmbH Vienna since 1997. Karmen studied tourism management in Austria, and became a certified trainer and consultant for tourism and regional development. Since 2006, she has been responsible for the project management of 'Alpine Pearls'. She supports the initiation, implementation, management and evaluation of local, national, transnational and EU projects. Her areas of specialisation are sustainable regional and tourism development in protected areas; concepts for tourism development and destination management; intra- and interregional co-operation and co-operation between enterprises and institutions; project management; organisation and human resources development, coaching; and feasibility studies. Contact: mentil@oear.at

Tanya MacLaurin is a professor at the College of Management and Economics, in the School of Hospitality and Tourism Management at the University of Guelph, Ontario, Canada. She teaches courses in safety and security in tourism, food tourism and foodservice management. Her research interests include food safety, food tourism, and consumer behaviour related to travel and tourism. Contact: tmaclaur@uoguelph.ca

Gianna Moscardo has qualifications in applied psychology and sociology and joined the School of Business at James Cook University in 2002. Prior to joining JCU, Gianna was the Tourism Research project leader for the CRC Reef Research for eight years. Her research interests include understanding how consumers, especially tourists, make decisions and evaluate their experiences, and how communities and organisations perceive, plan for, and manage tourism development opportunities. She has published extensively on tourism and related areas with more than 170 refereed papers or book chapters. Contact: gianna.moscardo@jcu.edu.au

Laurie Murphy lectures in the School of Business at James Cook University in the area of tourism, events and sports management. Laurie's research interests focus on improving tourism's contribution to regional communities with an emphasis on tourism marketing, including a focus on the backpacker market, destination image and choice, and more recently destination branding and tourist shopping villages. Laurie is on the editorial boards of both the *Journal of Travel Research* and the *Journal of Travel and Tourism Marketing* and serves on the Tourism Development and Marketing Strategic Advisory Committee for Townsville Enterprise. Contact: Laurie.Murphy@jcu.edu.au

Joram Ndlovu is a Senior Lecturer at the University of KwaZulu-Natal in South Africa. He has extensive experience in the Tourism and Hospitality education sector spanning more than twenty years. He is a renowned educator, academic and scholar. He has taught at the Bulawayo Polytechnic, Hotel School (Zimbabwe); Midlands State University (Zimbabwe); the Polytechnic of Namibia (Namibia) and North West University (South Africa) respectively. His research interests are diverse and include tourism education, slow tourism, tourism marketing, sustainable tourism and cultural and heritage tourism. Joram has published extensively in these areas and has authored a number of book chapters, conference presentations and papers in internationally acclaimed academic tourism journals. Contact: Ndlovuj1@ukzn.ac.za

Marianna Sigala is assistant professor at the University of the Aegean, Greece. Before joining the University of the Aegean, she had been lecturing at the Universities of Strathclyde and Westminster in the UK. Her interests include service management, Information and Communication Technologies (ICT) in tourism and hospitality, and e-learning. She has professional experience from the Greek hospitality industry and has contributed to several international research projects. Her work has been published in several academic journals and international conferences. She is a past President of EuroCHRIE and she has served on the Board of Directors of I-CHRIE, IFITT and HeAIS. Contact: m.sigala@aegean.gr

Dr. Camelia Tepelus is a corporate responsibility researcher and advocate with specialised expertise in children's rights. She is a Co-founder of TheCode.org, the most developed voluntary tool for child protection in tourism, elaborated by ECPAT advised by UNICEF and UNWTO, where she served as Secretariat Coordinator between 2001 and 2012. Camelia regularly provides training and technical assistance to governments, non- profits and international organisations (UNICEF, ILO, UNWTO, UN Global Compact, etc) on corporate responsibility and protection of children's rights. Since October 2012, she has been the ECPAT USA State Policy and Development Director, managing NY State policy and legislation projects, advising on CSR, program development, monitoring and reporting, including fundraising from foundations and institutional donors. Camelia is fluent in English, Spanish and Romanian and holds a BSc in Marketing (1999) from the Academy of Economical Sciences and a BSc in Engineering (1999) from the Politechnica University (Romania), an MSc of Environmental Sciences and Policy (2001) and a PhD (2008) on corporate social responsibility and human rights from Lund University (Sweden). Contact: camelia.te@gmail.com

Stephen Wearing is an Associate Professor at the University of Technology, Sydney (UTS). His research and projects are in the area of Leisure and Tourism Studies, with a PhD focused on sustainable forms of tourism. Stephen has taught at a variety of universities in his career before UTS, including Wageningen University, Netherlands; Newcastle and Macquarie Universities, Australia. In 2000 he received an excellence in teaching award (UTS) and in 2008 a National Teaching Award, while his teaching of international students at the World Leisure and Tourism's International Centre of Excellence (WICE) and Australian Conservation Training Institute (ACTI) has also been applauded. Contact: Stephen.Wearing@uts.edu.au

About the Editors

Pierre Benckendorff, PhD, is a Senior Lecturer and social scientist in the School of Tourism, The University of Queensland, Australia. He has more than 10 years of experience in education and research in the tourism field in Australia and internationally. Previous and current experience includes teaching and development of undergraduate and postgraduate curricula in introductory tourism management, tourist behaviour, international tourism, tourism transportation, tourism technologies, tourism futures and tourism analysis. He is also the Chair of Teaching and Learning at the School of Tourism and is responsible for coordinating a team of teaching and learning staff; quality assurance; and curriculum reviews of undergraduate and postgraduate coursework programs in tourism, hospitality and event management. Pierre has received a number of teaching and learning awards and commendations and in 2007 was awarded an Australian Carrick Citation for Outstanding Contributions to Student Learning. His research interests include consumer behaviour, the impact of new technologies on tourism, tourism education and tourism scholarship and epistemology. He has been a member of the BEST Education Network since 2007 and serves on the Executive Committee as the Chair of Knowledge Creation. Contact: p.benckendorff@uq.edu.au.

Dagmar Lund-Durlacher, PhD, is Head of the Department of Tourism and Service Management and Dean of the Undergraduate School at MODUL University Vienna, Austria. Prior to her appointment she directed a market research institute in Berlin (Germany) and headed a Master Program for Sustainable Tourism Management at the University for Sustainable Development Eberswalde (Germany). She completed her doctoral studies at the Vienna University of Economics and Business and held a Research fellowship at the Department of Hospitality Management, University of Central Florida, Orlando, USA, funded by the Fulbright Commission. She is a member of several Scientific Associations including ISTTE, AIEST, DGT and ÖGAF. She is the acting chair of the BEST (Building Excellence in Sustainable Tourism) Education Network and co-chairs the Advisory Board of TourCert, a CSR certification scheme for tour operators. Her current research interests focus on environmental management systems and eco certifications schemes for the tourism industry, climate change and sustainable transportation, green consumer behaviour, and corporate social responsibility. Contact: dagmar.lund-durlacher@modul.ac.at

Acknowledgements

The editors and case authors would like to acknowledge the assistance of Olivia Ruggles-Brise and Anja Eckervogt at the World Travel and Tourism Council who facilitated the relationships between case authors and representatives of the Tourism for Tomorrow Award winners and finalists as well as the invaluable support of David Leonard in proofreading earlier drafts of the book. We would also like to acknowledge Susann Kruegel, who initiated this idea with the BEST Education Network before departing the WTTC to commence a PhD. Many of the award winners and finalists represented in this volume have been very enthusiastic about sharing their stories and we would like to thank each of the organisations for sharing vital information with our authors. Finally, we would like to thank our authors, many of whom undertook to visit the case study sites using their own resources. This truly international collection of cases would not have been possible without the help of this cast of individuals who are all passionate about sustainable tourism.

1 Introduction

Pierre Benckendorff, *The University of Queensland*

Dagmar Lund-Durlacher, *MODUL University Vienna*

■ Background

International Cases in Sustainable Travel & Tourism is a joint initiative of the World Travel and Tourism Council (WTTC) and the Building Excellence in Sustainable Tourism Education Network (BEST Education Network). The WTTC is an international forum for business leaders which works to raise awareness of travel and tourism as one of the world's largest industries. The BEST Education Network is an international consortium of tourism educators and researchers committed to furthering the creation and dissemination of knowledge within the field of sustainable tourism.

The notion of sustainable tourism development has become a core principle in many tourism programs and degrees. The 1972 Stockholm Conference on the Human Environment and the 1980 World Conservation Strategy of the International Union for the Conservation of Nature (IUCN) created the momentum for the Brundtland Commission and the subsequent release of *Our Common Future* (or *The Brundtland Report*). *Our Common Future* defined the concept of sustainable development as "development that meets the needs of the present without compromising the ability of future generations to meet their own needs". This definition has been enthusiastically embraced by educators and some parts of the tourism industry who recognise that the survival of tourism relies on the quality of cultural and natural resources on which the industry depends. Despite this, sustainable development has been criticised as a vague concept. Brundtland's definition of sustainable development represents a threshold learning concept for learners but it remains a complex concept to grasp without clear examples in a range of different contexts.

This book includes a collection of contemporary international best practice cases, representing award winners and finalists from the WTTC Tourism for Tomorrow Awards. Since 2003, the WTTC Tourism for Tomorrow Awards have recognised best practice in sustainable tourism in four different categories:

Destination Stewardship, Conservation, Community Benefit and Global Tourism Business. Each year, winners are selected among 12 finalists by an international team of independent judges in each of the four award categories. Winning submissions need to successfully demonstrate sustainable tourism practices, including the protection of natural and cultural heritage, social and economic benefits to local people, and environmentally-friendly operations.

The purpose of this book is to supplement existing resources on the topic of sustainable tourism by providing a series of best-practice cases from around the world. The case studies provide a number of examples which can be used to transform the learning process from one that is abstract and uninspiring to one that is targeted and vibrant, which generates new insights, applies knowledge and encourages deep learning. It is not designed to be a standalone comprehensive introductory text. Rather, the cases will emphasise the concept of sustainable tourism and how sustainability can be incorporated into the phenomenon of tourism at the micro, meso and macro levels. It is suggested that this book should be used to accompany a core text or set of readings in sustainable tourism.

A key strength of the book is the inclusion of cases from a broad geographical range, with cases from both developing and developed countries in Europe, North America, Africa, Asia and Australasia. This reflects the fact that concepts and challenges of sustainability differ from one destination to another (see Figure 1.1). Cases are written by local scholars with an international reputation who are experts in sustainable tourism and who have first-hand knowledge of the cases through their local expertise. In some cases, representatives of the award winners and finalists have also contributed as authors to the case design.

Figure 1.1: Case study Locations

■ Organisation of the Book

The cases in the book were carefully selected to cover all four categories of the Tourism for Tomorrow awards. **Part I Destination Stewardship** contains four cases: *Alpine Pearls*, an association in the Alpine region aiming to develop environmentally friendly tourist mobility offers. The case focuses on the role of transport in holiday travel and the related environmental impacts as well as stakeholder management and communication. *The Okavango Delta Management Plan* presents a best practice example of stakeholders with different interests working together to develop an integrated resources plan for the famous Botswana Ramsar site. The *Montenegro* case focuses on a participatory approach as a means of empowering local and regional stakeholders in the sustainable development of tourism in the Bjelasica-Komovi region. The last case in Part I focuses on sustainable management strategies in a protected natural environment such as Australia's *Great Barrier Reef*. The case discusses how successful partnerships between the tourism industry and protected areas can be established. Stakeholder management and stewardship extended by collaborative partnerships, public participation, mutuality and government coordination are central concepts in the first four cases.

Part II focuses on **Global Tourism Business** and discusses the sustainable practises of three of the leading sustainable hotel corporations. The first case is about *Accor* and their focus on protecting children from trafficking and sexual exploitation. A variety of instruments and measures designed to combat child trafficking and sexual exploitation are described and the impacts these have had in strengthening the corporate brand and partnerships with a variety of stakeholders are discussed. The *Banyan Tree* case has a very different focus and is concerned primarily with environmental protection and conservation. The case develops an understanding of the role of entrepreneurship in strategic sustainable development and demonstrates best practice in environmental protection by describing the development of Laguna Phuket in Bang Tao Bay, Thailand. The corporate social responsibility (CSR) practices of *Marriott International* are discussed in the last case. The case discusses the ways sustainable business concepts and procedures have been implemented into Marriott's strategies and operations. All three of the cases in this section centre around the concept of corporate social responsibility including discussions on values, ethics, entrepreneurship, stakeholders and stewardship.

Part III covers two of the Tourism for Tomorrow Awards categories and comprises cases on **Conservation** and **Community Benefits**. The first case study examines the collaborative sustainable practices adopted by three vertically integrated and sister organisations in Zakynthos, Greece which aim to promote tourism development, while simultaneously protecting the marine life of the island. The case shows the importance of sustainable supply chain management as well as involving the customer in sustainable tourism. *Agritourism in India* describes the concept of agritourism in Indian rural areas and shows how this concept can contribute to community development and wellbeing. The coexistence of local communities and wildlife is discussed in the case of *Namibia's Communal Conservancy Tourism Sector*. The case provides insights into the strategies undertaken by the Namibian government to use tourism as an incentive for local communities to coexist with wildlife through communal conservancies. The last case, *Whale Watch Kaikoura* describes the successful development of an ecotourism business which is run by a local, indigenous community while at the same time meeting the requirements and guidelines of ecotourism, including those related to whale watching. All four of the cases in this section focus on community involvement as a central concept for sustainable tourism development.

■ For Instructors

All cases are presented in a logical and consistent structure which commences with a **synopsis** and an outline of the **learning outcomes.** The cases cover a range of **key concepts** which have been deliberately included to help students make the link between theory and practice. Table 1.1 provides an overview of the major sustainability concepts that can be found in each case and should offer a useful tool for instructors searching for the most appropriate cases. Theoretical considerations are followed by a **case analysis** and an outlook to the **future**. Each case includes a number of challenging **study questions** to help learners to consolidate and apply what they have learned.

The case study approach requires that the instructor becomes a facilitator. The aim is to provide learners with practical examples and problem solving experience so they can develop the skills needed for a successful career in tourism. With this in mind, the cases are supported by supplementary **instructor resources** available online from the publisher. A set of teaching notes for each case provides a synopsis, an outline of the learning outcomes, an explanation of the theoretical concepts underlying the case, additional readings, links to case relevant websites, tips and suggested teaching approaches and indicative answers to the study questions. A short PowerPoint presentation is also available online for each case.

■ For Learners

The cases presented in this book represent best practice examples of sustainable tourism in action and generally do not focus on a major problem or issue. However, study questions are provided at the end of each chapter to focus your thinking. It is suggested that these questions are best analysed through individual reflection or collaboration in small teams. It is useful to read the case several times, highlighting the key themes or concepts and developing your ideas by consulting additional resources such as readings and websites.

By focussing on destination stewardship, sustainable business, conservation and community benefits the book explores the complexities of sustainable development in the field. Although several introductory books offer brief cases to illustrate concepts in sustainable tourism development, this book provides in-depth cases that enable more advanced learners to apply theory to practice. The cases challenge learners to not only understand theory but also to apply it in practical contexts.

Table 1.1: Matrix of cases and key concepts

	Alpine Pearls	Okavango Delta	Montenegro	Great Barrier Reef	Accor	Banyan Tree	Marriott	Ionian Eco Villagers	Agritourism India	Namibia	Kaikoura
Carbon footprints							✓				
Collaborative partnerships				✓							
Community involvement								✓	✓	✓	✓
Core values						✓					
Corporate social responsibility					✓	✓	✓				
Ecotourism											✓
Entrepreneurship		✓				✓		✓	✓		
Ethics					✓		✓				✓
Government coordination				✓							
Mobility	✓										
Mutuality				✓							
Planning and strategy		✓			✓			✓		✓	
Poverty alleviation									✓		
Public participation				✓							
Resource management		✓		✓						✓	
Responsible consumption								✓			
Rural development									✓		
Stakeholders	✓	✓		✓	✓		✓	✓			
Stewardship	✓	✓	✓	✓	✓			✓			✓
Sustainable development				✓				✓	✓		
Tourist experience	✓										
Value chains					✓				✓		

INTERNATIONAL CASES IN SUSTAINABLE TRAVEL & TOURISM

PART 1

DESTINATION STEWARDSHIP

2 Alpine Pearls: A Network Promoting Environmentally Friendly Holidays

Dagmar Lund-Durlacher, *MODUL University Vienna*

Anja Hergesell, *MODUL University Vienna*

Karmen Mentil, *Alpine Pearls*

Synopsis and Learning Outcomes

Encouraging environmentally friendly transportation is seen as an important element of mitigating climate change and developing sustainable tourism. This case study provides a good example for developing and marketing environmentally friendly mobility options in order to reduce the environmental impacts caused by tourists' travel both to the holiday destination as well as in the destination.

The Alpine Pearls Association was established on 29 January 2006 by 17 members aiming to develop environmentally friendly tourist mobility options. The number of member destinations has since grown from 17 to 28. This case study will present the role of transport in holiday travel and will examine related environmental impacts. It then turns to stakeholder management and discusses the planning, development and marketing of environmentally friendly holiday options, the importance of stakeholder involvement as well as tools and instruments for stakeholder management and communication. Stakeholder theory (Freeman, 1984; Frederick *et al.*, 1992) will be discussed in the context of Alpine Pearls' network management by pointing out the important elements of successful stakeholder management such as the analysis of formal and informal relationships, of stakeholder interests and power relations and the development of integrative stakeholder programs. The case shows that successful international stakeholder management, including collaborative processes with democratic decision-making and transparent, respectful and trusting communication, can foster sustainable development beyond individual destinations and increase awareness and demand for environmentally friendly holidays.

After completing this case study, learners should be able to:

1   Understand the role of sustainable transportation in the provision of the tourism product.

2   Identify stakeholders and their role in delivering a sustainable tourist experience.

3   Analyse opportunities and challenges, and develop strategies to involve stakeholders for sustainable tourism development.

4   Recognise challenges and barriers to successful stakeholder management.

5   Explain the role of communication in successful stakeholder management.

■   Background

Alpine Pearls is an association of 28 Alpine destinations (see Figure 2.1), of which five are located in Austria, two in France, two in Germany, sixteen in Italy, one in Slovenia and two in Switzerland.

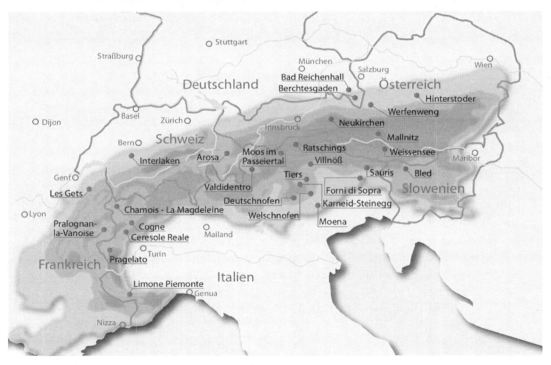

Figure 2.1: Member destinations of Alpine Pearls, *Source:* Alpine Pearls (n.d.)

2

Mobility concerns are at the heart of the Alpine Pearls' mission. The Alps are an important European transit region for both international trade and leisure travel between northern and southern Europe. At the same time, the Alps themselves are a very popular tourist destination attracting about 30 million international tourists (in 2006) and even more domestic tourists every year (Bartaletti, 2008). Indeed, including second homes, annual overnights in the region amount to 545 million making it the second most visited region worldwide after the Mediterranean coast (Bartaletti, 2008). Both trade and tourism (most domestic and continental tourists arrive by car (Peeters, 2004)) make heavy use of the few main roads to access or cross the Alps resulting in frequent traffic jams particularly during holiday season.

The volume of traffic in the European Alps impacts on the global environment as its emissions contribute to climate change, which in turn affects the attractiveness of the Alps as a winter destination due to decreases in snow fall as a result of temperature increases (Astelbauer-Unger *et al.*, 2011). Moreover, the emissions deteriorate the local air quality and cause noise pollution. Indirectly, the traffic and its infrastructure reduce the space available to flora and fauna, as well as to agriculture and other human activities. This means that while the traffic from tourists travelling to the European Alps signifies economic well-being, it also negatively affects the residents' quality of life and the tourist experience, thus lessening the attractiveness of the destination and ultimately threatening the economic well-being which it has brought.

Recognising the need for developing environmentally friendly tourism in the European Alps, Alpine Pearls has established an active network of stakeholders to develop environmentally friendly holiday packages and market the idea of sustainable tourism and transport. Their main initiatives focus on the promotion of environmentally friendly transport options for arrival and departure, the development of environmentally friendly transport services within and between the member destinations including shuttle services, and the provision of environmentally friendly activities in the destination like riding e-bicycles and horse-drawn carriages, driving electric cars, cross country skiing, hiking, horseback riding and more (see Appendix).

■ Key Concepts

Tourism is inherently linked to the movement of people as they move from the traveller **generating region** via the **transit route region** to the tourist **destination region** and back (Leiper, 1979). Considering the impacts of tourist movements to and from the destination but also within and between the destinations, **mobility** is an important concept in regards to sustainable tourism development.

A range of **actors** are involved in the delivery of tourist transportation. These are either directly involved (i.e. airlines, railway companies, bus companies and airports), or are indirectly linked to the provision of transport (i.e. transport authorities whose decisions on infrastructure, regulations and policies affect the attractiveness of each mode of transport for tourists). These actors can also be categorised according to the role they play in the generating region, the transit route region and the tourist destination region.

The complexity of interrelationships between actors increases when taking into account that transportation is just one part of the tourist product. The tourist product comprises all the goods and services the tourist consumes as part of the trip, i.e. in the traveller generating region, the transit route region and the tourist destination region (Middleton, 1989). The tourist product or experience is often unique to each tourist and is based on his or her individual consumption patterns. While the tourist consumes goods and services provided by a range of suppliers, the trip is likely to be perceived holistically as a **tourist experience** (Middleton, 1989). This perception has implications for tourism planning, development and marketing. Suppliers and other actors have to work together to develop satisfying tourist experiences on the one hand, and sustainable tourism on the other.

Actors aiming to pursue sustainable tourism planning and development thus increasingly include approaches to public participation and collaborative learning which calls for the involvement of a broad range of stakeholders. **Stakeholders** are defined as all "affected by the achievement of the organisation's objectives" (Freeman, 1984). Stakeholders can be divided into **internal stakeholders** who are responsible for managing an organisation internally, and **external stakeholders** who influence or are affected by the organisation. External stakeholders can be further divided into primary and secondary stakeholders. **Primary stakeholders** are groups with reciprocal relationships to the business organisation such as customers, suppliers and competitors. **Secondary stakeholders**, by contrast, influence or are affected by the organisation indirectly, but have no direct interaction (Frederick *et al.*, 1992).

Putting the stakeholder management concept into practice involves:

1 the identification of relevant stakeholders,

2 the analysis of their formal and informal relationships, their interests and power relations,

3 the development of a general strategy for the organisation and specific strategies for the stakeholders, and

4 the development of integrative stakeholder programs

(Freeman, 1984; Frederick *et al.*, 1992).

■ Case Analysis

Alpine Pearls is a cooperative marketing association which promotes the idea of soft (sustainable) mobility as well as specific sustainable holiday options offered by member destinations (known as Pearls). The association promotes options for visitors to reach member destinations without a car and provides information about accessing public transportation when visitors are at the destination. Member destinations must meet strict quality criteria (see Appendix), including reduced traffic in village centres, provision of transfer services, mobility without cars and environmentally friendly holiday choices. The cooperative structure allows member destinations to learn from each other and use marketing resources more effectively. Moreover, the association establishes international collaborations both with like minded organisations and suppliers of other tourism product components in order to maximise awareness, support product development and product distribution.

In the pursuit of their aims, Alpine Pearls works together with internal and external stakeholders concerned with offering environmentally friendly mobility solutions for travel to and from, in and between destinations. Adopting the stakeholder management concept, Alpine Pearls recognises and seeks to collaborate with a number of stakeholders (see Figure 2.2). The primary internal actors are the member communities, the Board of Directors and the Alpine Pearls Management.

The member destinations may either be members from the political sphere (i.e. they are represented by the local mayor) or from the tourism industry (i.e. they are represented by the local head of the Destination Marketing Organisation (DMO)). Each type of membership has its advantages and disadvantages. As the mayor and the local council are elected, changes in local government may affect a destination's relationship with Alpine Pearls. The most negative experience in this regard has led to one destination leaving the association as the new mayor could not be convinced of the association's benefits. In contrast, DMO representatives do not change frequently and, when they do, the work is handed over so that the new person is already aware of Alpine Pearls and the destination's membership in the association. DMO representatives are also more knowledgeable about tourism concerns, which makes them the experts and opinion leaders in tourism-related discussions during the annual General Assembly. In legal matters, conversely, it is the mayors and local governments that have the expertise. Moreover, the latter have the power to implement a range of policies to establish alternative mobility solutions in the destinations. This ability to act is particularly important as many actions related to product development have to be managed and financed by the destinations themselves.

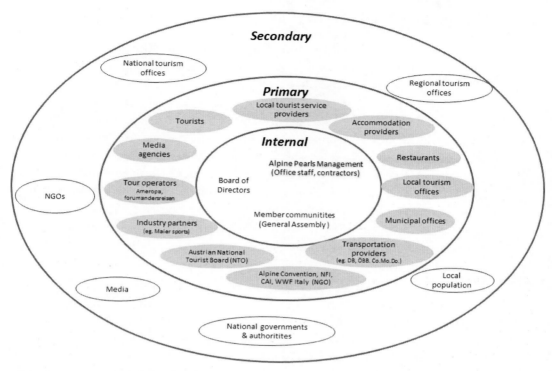

Figure 2.2: Alpine Pearls Stakeholders

The member destinations are represented in the General Assembly. That way, representatives of the members meet each other at least once a year. In addition, regular networking activities such as study trips and joint workshops support relationship building, the exchange of ideas and experiences and inter-destination learning. In addition to these face to face meetings, communication among members is facilitated by six newsletters per year which are distributed to the members' contact persons (about 120 addresses), as well as regular information on events and current activities via email. All these activities support the development of innovations in the destinations, on the one hand by learning about other destinations' initiatives, and on the other hand by encouraging the initiation of joint projects. Indeed, several member destinations collaborate in EU-funded projects.

The relationship between Alpine Pearls and its member destinations is formalised. The members have to pay a one-time entry fee and an annual fee of 12,000 EUR, which constitutes the budget for all marketing activities and for the maintenance of the Alpine Pearls Management. Moreover, the destinations have to comply with a list of criteria and have to prepare an annual report for internal quality control. The latter is important as the member destinations differ in their size, volume of tourist arrivals and overnights (see Figure 2.3) and the extent to which environmentally friendly tourist offers coexist next to traditional tourist offers. However, the compliance with the criteria (e.g. developing non-motorised areas in the destination and providing electrically generated vehicles) is difficult for some of the destinations as it requires additional funds which have to be (primarily) raised by the destination. Alpine Pearls does try to support the destinations by applying for EU project funds.

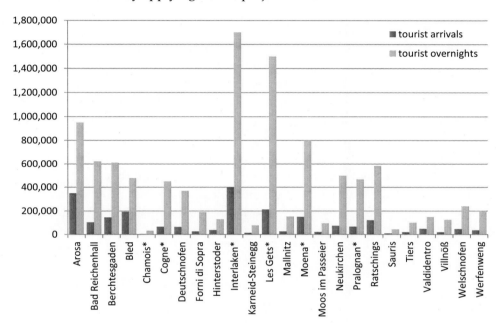

Note: The members that joined in 2012 and 2013 are not included in this overview. Numbers for these destinations are based on estimates or statistics of previous years

Figure 2.3: Number of tourist arrivals and overnights in 2010 by member destination.
Source: Based on table in Alpine Pearls, 2011

In exchange for the annual fee and compliance with the criteria, the member destinations are marketed by Alpine Pearls. This means that each member destination is presented on the association's website (http://www.alpine-pearls.com/en/) and destination holiday offers are available for booking. The members are also featured in the Alpine Pearls newsletter that is sent out to prospective customers. As part of other marketing activities, Alpine Pearls highlights the most innovative of its member destinations. This means that some degree of competition is fostered between members to develop innovative products. Moreover, branding of the destination as a member of Alpine Pearls is rewarded with a bonus system offering free additional internet promotion for that destination. Thus, each destination can increase the extent to which it is marketed by being an active member.

Each member destination is represented in the General Assembly which meets once a year and decides on the future strategies, the network's annual action plan (including marketing activities) as well as on the allocation of the budget to the respective activities. Each member community has one vote when decisions have to be taken. Every three years, the General Assembly elects the Board of Directors which consists of the president, 6 vice-presidents (one representative from each participating country) and one treasurer. Members of the Board of Directors all work on a voluntary basis, receiving no financial compensation. The Board meets four times a year, two times in person and two times via teleconference. The Board prepares annual balance sheets, issues invitations and prepares the General Assembly Meeting, reports to the General Assembly, supervises the Alpine Pearls Management and makes employment decisions. The president and his substitute also represent the association externally.

So far, the first president has been continuously re-elected. As such, Mr Brandauer from Austria has played a vital role in the development of the association. He has not only fulfilled the official duties of a president but has also acted as a successful mediator when member destinations have disagreed on issues. While his presidency has led the association to blossom, it has also led to German-speaking relationships dominating Alpine Pearls. Mr Brandauer recognises these disparities and has argued for the election of a new president from another member country.

The Alpine Pearls network is administered by the Alpine Pearls management team consisting of the Alpine Pearls Office and contractors and agencies that are used to undertake particular tasks. The Alpine Pearls Office is headed by the Executive Director who is appointed by the General Assembly. The Director, Karmen Mentil, is supported by two project assistants and two translators at the head office in Austria. Two additional staff members work in Italy and France where local offices have recently been established.

The management team coordinates all of Alpine Pearls' internal and external activities. Internally, the management team is, among other things, responsible for preparing the official meetings of the Board of Directors and the General Assembly, the preparation of the annual budget, activity plan and the annual report, as well as for coordinating and implementing the activities outlined in the annual activity plan. As part of the annual activity plan, the Alpine Pearls management team pursues the recruitment of new member destinations, at the time of writing, particularly in Germany and France as these countries are currently underrepresented. Furthermore, the management team is in charge of quality control. Next to checking the destinations' annual self-assessments, random external quality checks are conducted every year by contracting third party agencies. Finally, the management team is also responsible for ensuring internal communication.

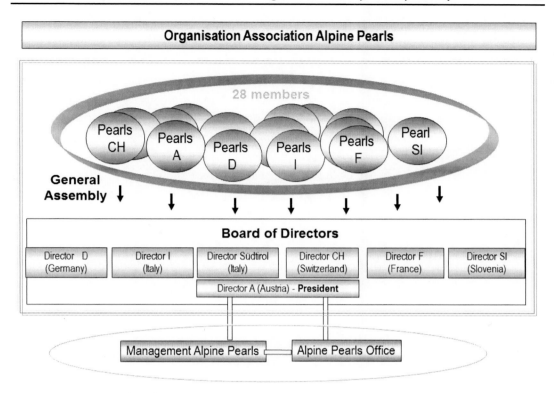

Figure 2.4: Organisational chart (adapted from Alpine Pearls)

Communication within the network is carried out in three languages, namely German, French and Italian, as not all members are fluent in one language. This regularly leads to misunderstandings despite the use of professional translators for meetings and informational materials. While professional translators know other languages, they are not always familiar with the linguistic repertoire of the respective industry. Concepts related to sustainable tourism and transportation are particularly difficult, both due to language use and national differences in conceptualisation of the terms. Moreover, the use of translators increases communication costs. Communication is thus considered the greatest challenge encountered by Alpine Pearls.

Externally, the Alpine Pearls office is responsible for raising awareness for sustainable tourism and transport and for marketing its member destinations to the national and international public by promoting their environmentally friendly transportation and fun mobility offers. The latter describes the use of environmentally friendly mobility activities for leisure purposes (e.g. driving Segways). Alpine Pearls thereby bundles the resources for marketing which enables its members to use their funds more effectively to reach a wider market. Alpine Pearls has a website on which the member destinations are featured and uses social media like Facebook, Twitter and YouTube. The online marketing comple-ments the traditional promotion work based on print materials such as informa-tion folders and occasional Alpine Pearls magazines. Member destinations are required to display the Alpine Pearls logo on all promotional material, including their website, in order to increase awareness and publicity. The association also prepares four pages of informational materials which the member destinations are asked to include in their brochures.

The Alpine Pearls management, in collaboration with three media agencies in Munich, Paris and Milan, runs image campaigns, organises press trips and hosts round-tables with experts to present the network's innovative mobility solutions and E-mobility. They regularly participate and present at conferences and other events, and promote their activities at fairs. E-newsletters in four languages are sent 4-6 times per year to a database of external recipients. The database is comprised of external contacts of the member destinations and contact details of prospective customers collected in competitions and quizzes with cooperation partners.

Strategic cooperation with external organisations is crucial in order to increase the efficiency and effectiveness of Alpine Pearls' activities. Most cooperation starts through personal contact and is based on verbal agreements rather than on formal written agreements.

In order to provide an environmentally friendly arrival to and departure from the destination, cooperation with transportation providers has been established. Transport infrastructure is nationally organised, which means Alpine Pearls has to cooperate with national railway companies. Due to different laws and regula-tions, this constitutes a major challenge, particularly for providing cross-border transportation solutions across the Alpine Pearls destinations. So far, Alpine Pearls has entered into cooperation with DB (German railway) and ÖBB (Austrian railway) and some regional railway companies like Co.Mo.Do. The cooperation focuses mainly on joint media and promotional activities.

Alpine Pearls also cooperates with German tour operators such as Ameropa, Mondial and ONE WORLD which create and distribute holiday packages to Alpine Pearls member destinations. While this could be viewed as a good opportunity for cross-marketing, the tour operators' frequently fail to explicitly inform Alpine Pearls about their decisions as to whom they have included in and excluded from their catalogues.

Cooperation with national tourist organisations has varied in success. While the Austrian National Tourism Board has supported Alpine Pearls with joint media and marketing activities, cooperation with the German National Tourist Office could not be established.

Cooperation with companies such as electro mobility vehicles, sports and leisure goods suppliers also provide many opportunities for cross-marketing. However, it has been difficult to enter cooperation in all member countries due to language barriers but also limited funds, as potential partners frequently require a financial contribution for joint marketing activities.

Cooperation with kindred organisations has been developed to build awareness and promote the initiatives of Alpine Pearls member communities in developing environmental friendly tourism. A memorandum of understanding has been signed with the Alpine Convention, which provides guidelines for sustainable development in the Alpine region. Further cooperation has been established with non-governmental organisations such as Nature Friends International.

Alpine Pearls not only wants to create and promote environmental friendly holidays; the association also strives to create environmentally and culturally sustainable member communities. While the local population benefits from the development of environmentally friendly transport solutions, Alpine Pearls also asks its members to actively promote the idea of sustainable development in their destinations. Several events such as themed days in local kindergartens and schools, workshops and discussion rounds for adults and celebrations of the European 'Car Free Day' are organised each year. Such initiatives have helped to create awareness about environmental issues and climate protection and have encouraged a change of attitudes and behaviours within the local communities.

■ Conclusions and Future Outlook

Alpine Pearls is the first international network in Europe that develops and markets environmentally friendly tourist mobility choices. The combined efforts of all stakeholders involved in this process have resulted in initial successes: the awareness of and demand for sustainable tourism options in the European Alps has increased and more guests are travelling to and from Alpine destinations by train. This progress is particularly attributable to successful stakeholder management. It builds on regular, open, respectful and trusting communication between all internal stakeholders and democratic processes in decision-making, as well as on continuously reaching out to external stakeholders in order to convince them of collaborative benefits.

Nevertheless, there are a range of challenges facing Alpine Pearls and its members. These challenges relate to stakeholder communication, product development and quality control. Communication is constrained by geographic distances and language barriers between member destinations. Furthermore the member destinations are heterogeneous in size, volume of tourists, the extent of resources available and the extent to which innovative mobility offers are provided. This makes it difficult to develop a standardised offer. This is exacerbated as the environmentally friendly mobility options coexist with traditional tourist offerings to varying degrees in the destinations, thereby threatening the credibility of Alpine Pearls and its member destinations as sustainable tourism providers.

Recognising these challenges, Alpine Pearls has committed itself to qualitative rather than quantitative growth. While it has ambitions to add another 10-15 member destinations (particularly in Germany, France and Slovenia, as these countries are currently underrepresented), it will only admit destinations with strong environmental profiles. Acknowledging the financial constraints of many communities and the need for investments to become environmentally friendly, Alpine Pearls supports applications for EU co-funding of projects by member destinations. Cooperation with external stakeholders for the development and distribution of environmentally friendly holiday offers will be pursued further in order for the member destinations to gain a competitive advantage among environmentally concerned tourists. Next to these immediate plans related to the network, Alpine Pearls envisions transferring the concept and the knowledge gained to other regions, creating similar networks around the world. Initial interest has already been indicated by destinations in Scandinavia and the Mediterranean.

■ Study Questions

1   Visit the website http://www.alpine-pearls.com/, choose 2-3 of the holiday packages on offer by clicking on the respective photos and discuss their environmental friendliness, considering the mobility aspects discussed in the case study and drawing on the criteria listed in the Appendix.

2   Identify the stakeholders of Alpine Pearls (internal and external) and describe their role in producing/delivering the tourist product/tourist experience.

3   How does Alpine Pearls involve stakeholders for sustainable tourism development in their member destinations? What problems could be encountered in this process? Consider differences in size, geographic spread and type of membership.

4   Describe the communication between the stakeholders (internal, external). What are the challenges to effective communication?

5   Discuss the challenges encountered by Alpine Pearls and its internal stakeholders. Form groups and develop ideas of how to address these challenges.

■   References

Alpine Convention (n.d.) 'The Convention', organisation's homepage, retrieved from http://www.alpconv.org/en/convention/default.aspx on 16 November 2012.

Alpine Pearls (2011) 'Massnahmenplan 2012: Marketing- und Kommunikation Budget', internal document, Werfenweng, Austria: Alpine Pearls.

Alpine Pearls (n.d.) 'Alpine Pearls – Holidays in Eco-Motion', organisation's homepage, retrieved from http://www.alpine-pearls.com/en/home.html on 16 November 2012.

Alps Mobility (n.d.) 'Alps Mobility I and Alps Mobility II', EU project website, retrieved from www.alpsmobility.net/main_frame.htm?uk on 16 November 2012.

Astelbauer-Unger, K., Baumgartner, C., Hrbek, R. & Plattner, G. (2011) 'Alpiner Wintertourismus und Klimawandel', Nature Friends International website, retrieved from www.naturfreunde.at/files/uploads/2012/01 on 16 November 2012.

Bartaletti, F. (2008) 'What Role Do the Alps Play within World Tourism?', CIPRA organisation, retrieved from alpsknowhow.cipra.org/background_topics/alps_and_tourism/alps_and_tourism_chapter_introduction.html on 15 November 2012

Co.Mo.Do. (n.d.) 'Ferrovie dimenticate', organisation's homepage, retrieved from http://www.ferroviedimenticate.it on 16 November 2012.

Frederick, W.C., Post, J.E. and Davis, K. (1992) *Business and Society – Corporate Strategy, Public Policy, Ethics*, New York: McGraw-Hill.

Freeman, R.E. (1984) *Strategic Management: A Stakeholder Approach*, Mansfield, MA: Pitman.

Hemmati, M. (2001) *Multi-Stakeholder Processes for Governance and Sustainability – Beyond Deadlock and Conflict*, London: Earthscan, retrieved from http://www.earthsummit2002.org/msp/book.html on 20 May 2012.

Jamal, T. & Getz, D. (1995) 'Collaboration theory and community tourism planning', *Annals of Tourism Research*, **22** (1), 186-204.

Leiper, N. (1979) 'The framework of tourism: towards a definition of tourism, tourist, and tourist industry', *Annals of Tourism Research*, **6** (4), 390-407.

March, R. & Wilkinson, I. (2009) 'Conceptual tools for evaluating tourism partnerships', *Tourism Management*, **30**, 455-462.

Middleton, U. (1989) 'Tourist product', in S.F. Witt & L. Moutinho (eds.), *Tourism Marketing and Management Handbook*, London: Prentice Hall, pp. 572-576.

Nature Friends International (n.d.) Nature Friends International homepage, retrieved from http://www.nfi.at//index.php?lang=en on 16 November 2012.

Peeters, P., Van Egmond, T. and Visser, N. (2004) European tourism transport and environment, Second draft deliverable 1 for the DG-ENTR MusTT project, prepared by NHTV Centre for Sustainable Tourism and Transport, retrieved from http://www.cstt.nl/userdata/documents/appendix_deliverable_1_subject_matter_review_30082004.pdf on 15 November 2012.

Verbeek, D.H.P., Bargeman, A. & Mommaas, J.T. (2011) 'A sustainable tourism mobility passage', *Tourism Review*, **66** (4), 45-53.

Appendix: Alpine Pearls' Member Criteria

Alpine Pearls has a list of criteria particularly related to mobility as a means of transport (between traveller generating regions and destinations, as well as between destinations) and mobility as a fun activity.

Regulatory criteria:

- The community must explicitly commit itself to the principles of sustainability.
- The community must explicitly commit itself to fulfilling the member criteria.
- If there are deficiencies in the compliance with criteria, the destination must show in measurable terms that it is aiming to overcome this deficiency.
- Tourism must play a central role in the community. This is measured either by average number of overnights over three years, number of inhabitants related to number of overnights, or number of inhabitants related to bed capacity.
- The community must have passed an environmentally friendly mobility development concept in the destination.
- No heavily used streets (i.e. more than 10,000 vehicles/day) may be located in the destination's centre.
- The destination must have areas only for pedestrians, like parks etc. If the destination is a town/city, it must have pedestrian areas and areas of little traffic.
- The destination must be typical in architecture and character for the region. No factories and companies causing noise pollution are allowed in the destination.

Mobility as a means of transport:

- There must be transportation solutions available for people who arrive by train/bus or who do not want to use their car at the destination.
- Transportation must be offered with vehicles of the newest technology. Environmentally friendly vehicles should be used if possible.
- All offers must accommodate the special needs of mobility impaired customers.
- The destination must be accessible without a car every day of the week from 8am to 10pm. At least one of the following services must be available at least every 2 hours:
  - ❑ Bus/train
  - ❑ Shuttle service between the destination and the nearest bus/train station with long distance connections
  - ❑ Taxis
- Destinations must ensure a high quality in the travel to/from the destination by ensuring luggage transport and a maximum waiting time of 15 minutes between arrival at the station and pick up for transport to the destination.
- The destination must be connected to the regional public transport network, so that all attractions can be reached daily without a car.

- The frequency of the service depends on customer needs but should ensure regular services during the weekend and optimal connectivity between modes of transport.
- A map showing the regional public transport network must be offered to all tourists.
- If there is no adequate public transport network, the community must establish an alternative network of shuttle buses.
- Within the destination, an environmentally friendly transport system must be in place. It can include buses, trains, horse carriages and cable cars. The offer must be available every day of the week. Guests arriving without car and those not wishing to use it in the destination should have free use of the transport system included in their guest cards. Destinations, in which all attractions can be reached on foot, do not need to offer a local transport system.

Mobility as a fun activity:

- The destination is not allowed to offer motor sports activities. All activities on offer should be environmentally friendly such as hiking, (Nordic) walking, mountain climbing, cycling, mountain biking, swimming, rowing, horseback riding, driving electrically powered vehicles, paragliding, skiing, snowboarding, ice-skating and sledding.
- Each destination must offer a minimum of fun mobility activities, namely hiking trails, at least one hire for bikes and for electrically-run vehicles. Moreover, the destination must specialise in at least one stream of mobility activities (e.g. hiking, horseback riding or skiing – see activities listed above).

Further criteria relate to:

- Information requirements to make customers, tourism providers and residents aware of sustainability and the environmentally friendly offers for transport and fun;
- Ensuring the quality of the tourism product, the tourist experience and the environment;
- Saving energy and using regional produce along the value chain;
- Sustaining the cultural and architectural uniqueness of the region;
- Adopting participatory planning approaches.

3 Planning for Sustainability:
The Okavango Delta Management Plan

Haretsebe Manwa, *North West University*

Synopsis and Learning Outcomes

Integrated management plans are paramount for ensuring the sustainability of resources which have many stakeholders, such as the Okavango Delta in Botswana. The Okavango Delta is the largest Ramsar site. Ramsar refers to the Convention on Wetlands of international importance. It is an intergovernmental treaty that mandates member states to conserve and use wetlands wisely through local, regional and national actions and international cooperation as a contribution towards achieving sustainable development throughout the world (Ramsar, 2013a). The Okavango Delta is also one of the largest inland deltas and a World Heritage site. Signatories to the Ramsar Convention are expected to develop and implement plans for designated Ramsar sites to promote conservation of the wetlands in their respective countries.

In compliance with the Ramsar requirements, the Botswana Government launched the Okavango Delta Management Plan (ODMP) in 2002 and it was completed in 2007. The aim was to "develop a comprehensive integrated management plan for the conservation and sustainable use of the Okavango Delta and surrounding areas"(Department of Environmental Affairs, 2008). Consequently, the plan was designed to provide a framework and contextual guidelines for existing and future individual area and sector plans.

The case study presents the planning process followed in the development of the ODMP to highlight best practices in integrated resources management. The process shows how stakeholders with different interests were brought together and their views and interests incorporated in the formulation of the plan. Lessons learned from the planning process, for example the importance of open communication channels between stakeholders, especially local communities who normally do not have a voice in planning processes, are highlighted to show how the process has empowered stakeholders and given them confidence in planning activities. Whilst the ODMP plan formulation can be credited as being a product of thorough stakeholder input and support, there are still a lot of challenges facing the successful implementation of the ODMP including the role of other riparian states (Angola and Namibia), centralisation of decision making and structural challenges, financial mechanisms, competing priorities at the national level and selling the plan.

After studying this case, learners should be able to:

1   Understand and apply stakeholder theory to analyse the complexities of integrating stakeholders in the development of the Okavango Delta Management Plan.

2   Apply an integrated planning approach as stipulated by the Ramsar Convention to evaluate the Okavango Delta Management Planning process.

3   Propose appropriate strategies for the successful implementation of the Okavango Delta Management Plan.

■ Background

Botswana has for a long time relied on its mineral wealth, especially diamonds. Over the years the government has sought alternative ways of diversifying its economy. Tourism has therefore been identified as an alternative engine of growth and is currently the second greatest contributor to foreign currency earnings after mining (Government of Botswana, 2003). Among the Southern African Development Community (SADC) members, tourism has grown significantly in the past years as reflected in Table 3.1. In 2007, Botswana was ranked third in terms of arrivals among the SADC countries, but in terms of receipts it was ranked fourth. In addition, tourism contributes 6% of the country's Gross Domestic Product and 10.3% of total employment in Botswana, or 1 in every 9 jobs (WTTC, 2007).

The Okavango Delta in the North West of Botswana is a competitive tourist destination in the Botswana market, contributing over 6.5 per cent of Botswana's GDP. The Okavango River Basin is shared by three riparian states, Angola, Botswana and Namibia. Angola is upstream from Namibia, while Botswana is downstream (see Figure 3.1). The Okavango Delta Ramsar site covers an area of around 55,374 square kilometres (Magole, 2008). The Okavango Delta is a diverse and ecologically rich ecosystem. 147 species of mammals, 188 of trees, 570 of birds and 2150 of plants are currently known to exist in an environment comprising seasonal floodplains, lagoons, dry grassland, mopane forests and palm islands (Barnes *et al.*, 2006).

Table 3.1: International tourism arrivals and receipts in SADC countries 2005-2007

Country	International Arrivals (1000 arrivals)			International Receipts (US$ Million)		
	2007	2006	2005	2007	2006	2005
Angola	194	121	2010	-	75	88
Botswana	1455	1425	1474	546	537	562
Lesotho	300	357	304	-	36	31
Madagascar	344	312	277	176	159	183
Malawi	714	638	438	-	24	24
Mauritius	906	788	761	1299	1007	871
Namibia	-	833	778	434	384	348
Seychelles	161	141	129	285	228	192
South Africa	9090	8396	7369	8418	7875	7327
Swaziland	870	873	839	-	74	78
Tanzania	692	628	590	1037	950	824
Zambia	897	757	669	-	110	98
Zimbabwe	-	2287	1559	-	338	99

Source: UNWTO (2008) cited in Manwa (2011).

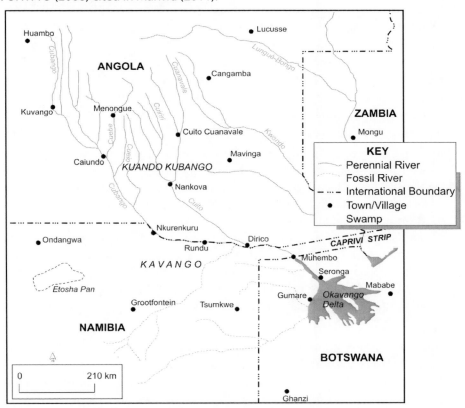

Figure 3.1: Location of the Okavango Delta

The area is a source of livelihood for local communities who harvest building reeds and thatching grass while practicing grazing, crop production and fishing activities. In addition, tourism is a significant economic activity in the Okavango Delta. The macro-economic impact of the Delta is reflected in Table 3.2. Total impact on GNP is estimated at 1.2 billion Pula, the currency of Botswana, which is approximately US$141million. It is estimated that between 18 and 31 per cent of this value enriches the poor either through Community Based Natural Resource Management (CBNRM) or direct employment.

Table 3.2: Macro-economic impact of the Okavango delta

2005	Direct GNP (1000 Pula)	Income multiplier (1000 Pula)	Indirect + Indirect GNP (1000 Pula)
RAMSAR SITE			
Tourism	400,970	2.58	1,032,870
Agriculture/natural resource use	73, 600	2.03	149,340
WETLAND			
Tourism	362,540	2.58	936,190
Agriculture/natural resource use	16,990	1.64	27,810
TOTAL WETLAND	379,530		964,000

Source: Barnes *et al.* (2006).

The Okavango Delta was designated as a Ramsar site in accordance with the International Convention for the Preservation of Wetlands in April 1997, thereby imposing a set of obligations which must be adhered to. For the purpose of this case study, these requirements will be divided into requirements applying to individual countries and those applying to international cooperation where resources are shared by more than one country. Individual countries are expected to:

> work towards the wise use of their wetlands through a wide range of actions and processes contributing to human well-being through sustainable wetlands water allocation and river basin management including for example, establishment of national wetlands policies, harmonising the framework of laws and financial instruments affecting wetlands, undertaking inventory and assessment, ensuring public participation in wetland management and the maintenance of cultural values by local communities and indigenous people; promoting communication, education, participation and awareness and increasing private sector involvement (Ramsar Secretariat, 2013).

Ramsar (2013b) also mandates international cooperation where resources are shared by multiple states as is the case with the Okavango Delta (i.e. Angola, Botswana and Namibia). In such cases, member states are required to cooperate in the conservation and sustainable use of the shared wetland water resources by putting in place sustainable management practices. In addition, they are to collaborate with other conventions and international organisations by sharing information and expertise and increasing the flow of financial resources and relevant technologies to less developed countries.

The Botswana Government has regional and national initiatives in place to comply with the Ramsar requirements. These include:

1 Permanent Okavango River Basin Water Commission of 1994 (OKACOM)
2 Botswana's Vision 2016 (Long-term Vision for Botswana, 1997)
3 The Draft Botswana National Wetlands Policy of 2002
4 Ngamiland District Development Plan

Permanent Okavango River Basin Water Commission of 1994 (OKACOM)

This agreement was reached among riparian states of the Okavango River basin to set up a permanent joint commission, known as OKACOM, to drive the operationalisation of the sustainable management of Okavango River basin resources for the benefit of its people.

Botswana's Vision 2016 (Long-term Vision for Botswana, 1997)

This is the aspiration of what Botswana should achieve by the year 2016, in line with UN Millennium Development Goals. Vision 2016 is based on seven pillars:

- an educated and informed nation;
- a prosperous, productive and innovative nation;
- a compassionate, just and caring nation;
- a safe and secure nation;
- an open, democratic and accountable nation;
- a moral and tolerant nation;
- an educated and proud nation.

Of greatest relevance to this case is the pillar which emphasises "a prosperous, productive and innovative nation". This pillar emphasises among other things: "equity in economic participation, sustainable use of natural resources, particularly non-renewable natural resources". Another important element of the pillar is the recognition of the role of communities in the sustainability of natural resources where they are expected to be at the forefront of the use, exploitation and management of natural resources, wildlife management and appreciation of the importance of a clean environment. As far as the Okavango Delta is concerned, the vision emphasises: "an urgent need to carry out an integrated environmental study to obtain data that could be used to form an Okavango Delta master plan. Such a plan must be sensitive to the socio-economic needs and development of the communities in the Delta whilst exploiting the immense tourism potential". In addition the Vision acknowledges the risks to the flow of water in the Okavango Delta that require joint management with neighbouring states.

☐ ## The Draft Botswana National Wetlands Policy of 2002

This policy was the result of extensive national consultation, which culminated in a national wetlands conference in 1994. The key issues raised by the policy included the urgency of compiling a national wetlands inventory so that appropriate management and conservation of these resources could be developed. The policy recommends the adoption of an ecosystem approach to the utilisation, conservation and management of wetlands and that plans should be developed which emphasise ecologically sustainable wetlands conservation. The policy further states that: "management plans will be drafted for all designated Ramsar sites and wetlands identified as nationally important". This policy culminated in the development of the Okavango Delta Management Plan which is the focus of this case study.

☐ ## Ngamiland District Development Plan

The vision of this plan is to strive for the development of a world-class nature-based tourism destination that is economically sustainable and optimises benefits to local communities and the nation within agreed limits of acceptable change. The plan emphasises the importance of livelihood improvement and sustainable management of the Okavango Delta in line with the requirements of the Ramsar convention. One of the problems of this plan was ownership. The plan lacked stakeholder involvement and support since consultation was limited to consultants and the land board. It is therefore prudent to come up with a plan in which all stakeholders have a buy-in.

■ # Key Concepts

The Okavango Delta Management Planning process typifies sustainable tourism management where **stakeholder collaboration** in **integrative planning** set the direction and limits of growth to the Okavango Delta, Botswana. It is generally recognised that tourism has the potential to destroy the very resources it depends on. For tourism development to be successful in the long term it must be planned and managed in a sustainable manner (Inskeep, 1991; Ruhanen, 2008). Sustainability is enshrined in the Okavango Delta Vision statement for tourism development, which states: "to strive for the development of a world class nature based tourism destination that is economically sustainable and optimises benefits to local communities and the nation within agreed limits of acceptable change" (Department of Environmental Affairs, 2006: 2).

Concerns with the **sustainability of tourism** have been of interest to researchers for a long time. However, there is still no agreement among academics on definition of sustainable tourism (Sharpley, 2000; Liu, 2003; Saarinen, 2006). The working definition is that of the World Tourism Organisation (1997: 30) which defines sustainable tourism: "is envisaged as leading to management of all resources in such a way that economic, social, and aesthetic needs can be fulfilled while maintaining cultural integrity, essential ecological processes, biological diversity, and life support systems". Cooper et al (2008:16) highlight an important element of sustainable tourism whereby they propose that sustainability should result in the long term economic, environmental, socio-cultural and political well-being of all stakeholders.

There are several definitions of **stakeholders** beyond the scope of this chapter (Sheehan &Ritchie, 2005). The definition adopted here is Freeman's (1984, cited in Kimbu &Ngoasong, 2013:237) who defined a stakeholder as "any group or individual who can affect or is affected by" tourism development in an area. The basic tenets of the stakeholder are power, legitimacy, proximity and urgency/ relevance (Mitchell *et al.*, 1997, cited in Sheehan &Ritchie, 2005). According to Freeman, wielding power without legitimacy does not necessarily define a person as a stakeholder. Proximity to the organisation or project has a direct impact on those communities whose livelihoods depend on the plan or project. Urgency is a function of time which affects the planning process in as far as those stakeholders who are affected need resolution of the planning in a beneficial outcome. (Sheehan &Ritchie, 2005).

In the Okavango Delta, the stakeholders are riparian communities, resource managers (government institutions), policy makers (Botswana Government, SADC/OKACOM), local non-governmental organisations, local communities, the business community (tourism and other sectors), international partners, other Riparian States, Ramsar, etc. tourists and researchers (Magole, 2008; Arntzen, 2005) (see Table 3.3). The Okavango Delta is very much dependent on the inflow of water from upstream in other countries like Angola and Namibia. Any developments that affect such water flow must be part of the shared goals of the plan for all stakeholders. This brings in the international third parties and the rules and regulation of dealing with shared resources.

Integrative planning is a mechanism of ensuring collaboration of stakeholders in planning and management (Farrell & Twining-Ward, 2005; Mill & Morrison, 1998). By its nature tourism involves interactions and joint operations with other systems that influence the sustainability of tourism (Farrell & Twining-Ward, 2004). Bramwell and Lane (1993) argue that sustainability holds promise to address the problems of negative tourism impacts and its long term viability. There is a need to limit and control tourism growth to guarantee its sustainability. A number of measurements have been developed to determine the capacity of destinations to ensure the sustainability of tourism. These include carrying capacity and limits of acceptable change (LAC). The Botswana Government, in the case of the Okavango Delta, has adopted the limits of acceptable change, which is a framework for establishing acceptable and appropriate resource and social conditions in recreation settings (Stankey *et al.*, 1984). The LAC represents a reformation of the recreational carrying capacity concept, with primary emphasis on the conditions desired in the area, rather than on how much use an area can tolerate (Ahn *et al.*, 2002).

■ Case Analysis

The many stakeholders with competing interests at local, national, regional and international levels, the Ramsar Convention, as well as the national and regional/international policies that Botswana is a signatory to, necessitated the development of an integrated plan for the Okavango Delta. This resulted in the Okavango Delta Management Plan (ODMP) (Department of Environmental Affairs, 2008). The formulation of the plan started in 2002 and was completed in 2007. The project was financed by the Botswana Government jointly with the **International Union for Conservation of Nature (IUCN),** the **Swedish Development agency (SIDA),** the **German Department of Economic Development (DED)** and the **Danish Development Agency (DANIDA).**

The ODMP is an integrated water and land resource management plan for the Okavango Delta Ramsar site. The aim is to develop a comprehensive, integrated management plan for the conservation and sustainable use of the Okavango Delta and surrounding areas, using the ecosystem approach which advocates stakeholder involvement in the management of natural resources. The detailed Vision, Mission and objectives of ODMP are attached in Appendix 1.

□ The Planning Process

The planning process deviated from the normal Botswana Development plan formulation, which is an exclusive domain of the relevant ministries. The coordinating department was Environmental Affairs under the Ministry of Wildlife, Environment and Tourism. The ODMP was driven by stakeholders based on their use and interest in the Okavango Delta's resources. The multiple uses of the resources resulted in 12 components being identified which became the task groups (poverty among communities, disjointed management of resources, animal and human diseases, skewed distribution of benefits from water resources, natural resource use conflicts, extreme water events)(see Magole (2008) and Mfundisi (2008) for a full description of the task teams).

The task groups, composed of experts in the identified area, were led by a relevant government department which provided technical support and drafted terms of reference for the team. For example the water-related task group included hydrologists, sociologists and other such experts in water and was coordinated by the Department of Water Affairs. The resource persons to spearhead the process were external consultants appointed for the purpose. The task teams were mandated to take a situational analysis of their sector by answering questions such as:

- What is the state of the resource?
- Who is using the resource?
- Who is managing the resource?
- Who else has an interest in the resource?

In addition to situational analysis, task teams were to use the ecosystem approach to resource management by answering some of the following questions:

- What role can you play in the planning process?
- What impact are you going to have during planning and implementation?
- Who will be affected by the ODMP?
- Are the existing plans relevant? What lessons can we learn from these plans?
- How do you want the Delta to look like in the future?

Table 3.3: Okavango Delta Ramsar Site Stakeholders

Type of Stakeholder	Characteristics	List of Stakeholders
Primary (125,000 people)	Direct dependency on natural or cultural resources Inhabitants of the Delta Small-scale commercial use	Community-based organisations, Village Development Committees, Farmers' Committees, Community trusts, Village Trust Committees
Secondary	Individuals indirectly dependent on the resources	Upstream communities, NGOs, Tour operators based in the Delta
Tertiary	Group of individuals with an interest in or influence over the OD Not dependent upon OD for livelihood People responsible for the management of the OD	Government, researchers, etc.

Source: Mfundisi *(2008)*

A parallel process was also run where consultations with primary stakeholders were held in order to benefit from indigenous knowledge to map out issues important for them to be included in the plan. Rural sociologists were engaged to spearhead the process. Issues arising from the community meetings were classified into the identified 12 components (task teams) and referred to relevant task teams for deliberation and consideration. Conversely, issues coming out of task team proceedings were referred to the primary stakeholders to deliberate on through rural meetings known as *Kgotlas*. Mfundisi (2008) states that 33 such meetings were held with communities between 2003 and 2004. An inception report was produced in November 2004 which provided a situational analysis, outlining issues important to different stakeholders as well as ecosystem characterisation. The respective government departments/organisations were given the responsibility of ensuring that the plan fully addressed issues identified under each component. The coordinators from each relevant government organisation reported to a steering committee of permanent secretaries and directors of the departments involved as task team coordinators. At the district level, the coordinators and the planning sectors reported to the Okavango Delta Wetland Management committee.

☐ Project Implementation

The implementation strategy for the ODMP follows the normal Botswana Government planning process, as shown in Table 3.4. The coordinating authority is the Department of Environmental Affairs which delegates responsibilities to the sectoral departments and institutions. The implementation follows a normal 6-year Botswana Government planning cycle which is aligned to the District Development Planning and National Development planning processes. However, no financial resources have been specifically allocated for implementation of the plan. Rather, activities have to compete for resources against other departmental projects.

Table 3.4: ODMP Implementation strategy

Coordinating Authority	Department of Environmental Affairs
Implementing Agencies	Sectoral Departments and Institutions
Planning Horizon	6 year Planning Cycle in line with District Development Plans and National Development Plan Processes
Plan Implementation	ODMP to be mainstreamed into normal District Development Plans and National Development Plans
Financial Resources	Financial resourcing through normal government budgetary procedures
Plan Review	Aligned with review of District Development Plans and National Development Plans

☐ Challenges

In addition to the policy frameworks, there were also pertinent management issues which needed urgent attention. Some of the issues that have been identified include the following:

- Poverty levels in Ngamiland
- Pressure on natural resources due to increasing demands (for reeds, thatching grass, fisheries, etc.)

- Land degradation from livestock and wildlife (e.g. elephants)
- Invasive alien species (e.g. Salvinia molesta)
- Competing commercial and traditional use interests, leading to conflicts between different use groups (e.g. the tourism industry and local communities, sports and subsistence fishers)
- Traditional land and resource rights not being fully defined and documented, and consequently not well protected
- Human-wildlife conflicts (e.g. elephant damage to crops and livestock predation)
- Unknown and poorly predictable consequences of climate change
- Limited information and data management to inform planning
- Undirected strategy for tourism industry (lacking citizen participation, management of growth and impacts on the environment)
- Overall value of an 'intact Delta' never assessed
- Trans-boundary, fugitive resources (water and wildlife)
- Upstream developments (Angolan repopulation, agriculture, hydropower, etc.)
- Pressure on natural resources due to increasing demands, competing commercial and traditional use interests, upstream developments and limited information and data management to inform planning.

Numerous studies have highlighted these issues (Mbaiwa, 2003, 2005, 2008), a few of which are discussed in more detail in the following paragraphs.

Competing commercial and traditional use

The Okavango Delta is a prime tourist destination. This has given rise to demand for pristine land for tourism development. Botswana Tourism Organisation records shows that there are about 107 camps and lodges and 71 mobile safari operators in the Okavango Delta, plus several community-based tourism organisations. Clashes occur between tourism operators and communities who would like to graze their livestock on the land occupied by tourism facilities (Mbaiwa *et al.*, 2008).The Government of Botswana, through legislation, has placed restrictions on other land use forms to ensure that they do not conflict with wildlife and its utilisation (Wildlife Conservation Policy, Tourism Policy of 1990, etc.). These regulations have alienated indigenous people, the Basarwa, whose traditional livelihoods hinge around the hunting and gathering of veldt products (Darkoh & Mbaiwa, 2009). The policing of restrictions on wildlife use by the Department of Wildlife and National Parks (DWNP) has negatively impacted communities in the Okavango Delta region since the area is one of the richest in wildlife resources in Botswana (Mbaiwa *et al.*, 2008).

Spread of HIV/AIDS

The Okavango Delta, like the rest of Southern Africa, is battling with the spread of HIV/AIDS, which is decimating the younger and active population. The HIV/AIDS pandemic in the Okavango Delta has resulted in a loss of employment owing to morbidity and mortality of prime-age adults and a drain on financial resources such as the costs of medical fees and funerals (Kgathi *et al.*, 2007).

Human wildlife conflict

The National Development Plan 9 (2003) acknowledges that human-wildlife conflict occurs in tourist destination areas. Communities in the Okavango Delta have cleared around 10,200 hectares for arable farming, of which 75% is used for the dry-land farm ing of sorghum and millet and the remaining 25% for *Molopo* (strip riverbank cultivation) farming of maize (Arntzen, 2005). Wildlife inflicts damage on livestock, crops and other community property, leading farmers to complain about an increase in crop damage by elephants and predation by wild animals including hyenas and lions. There is a feeling among communities that compensation from Government is inadequate (Atlhopheng and Mulale, 2009; Kgathi *et al.*, 2012).

As well as the policies discussed in this section, management issues justify urgency in coming up with a plan which involves all stakeholders. The Okavango Delta Management Plan was therefore an integrated management plan which involved all key stakeholders in the planning process.

■ Future Outlook

The Okavango Delta Management Plan is a step in the right direction. The plan formulation has been a collective effort by all key stakeholders. This is something that the other two riparian states could emulate. However, the successful implementation of the plan is dependent on effective management and collaboration with the other riparian states. Angola has embarked on reconstruction efforts through upstream developments including irrigation to revive the agricultural sector and hydro-electric power generation. These developments are likely to impact on the delta and its sustainability (Pinheiro *et al.*, 2003). The government of Botswana can use the OKACOM platform to persuade Angola and Namibia to develop relevant plans.

Key decisions that affect ecosystem management at the local level are being taken at the national level, for example tourism management strategies. In addition, financing mechanisms required for implementation are dependent on individual ministerial support. Because the ODMP is placed under the coordination of Department of Environmental Affairs, it is likely to receive only cursory attention in resource allocation decisions since the environment is not seen as a priority by government departments (Magole, 2008). During the project review, issues of financing the plan can be raised with relevant government departments to prioritise the implementation of the plan. In addition, the plan recognises the importance of capacity building at institutional and community levels in order to enhance understanding, dispel misconceptions, and create opportunities for sustainable use and management of the Okavango Delta resources. The ODMP project had allocated funds for this, but sectors should continue to budget annually for training and capacity building programmes which are relevant for the advancement of their ODMP implementation.

■ Summary and Conclusion

The Okavango Delta Management Plan is an effort to ensure that the Okavango Delta remains a vibrant tourist attraction and a conservation success. One of the key success factors of the plan is the buy-in of all stakeholders. The ODMP process has revealed a number of lessons that maybe useful for similar destinations to facilitate integrative planning processes. For example, developing institutional structures to facilitate coordination and integration, adopting an issue-driven approach which ensures broad-based stakeholder support and acceptance, providing coordination and technical advice through community indigenous knowledge systems and technical experts, ensuring continuous communication, and offering training and capacity building for institutions and stakeholders.

■ Study Questions

1 Debate the stakeholder theory and identify likely conflicts among stakeholders. Also show why stakeholders play an important role in achieving sustainable tourism development.

2 Identify the key stakeholders of the Okavango Delta. What were their roles in the Okavango Delta Management planning process? What are the likely challenges in integrating stakeholders' interests in the Okavango Delta Management planning process?

3 Familiarise yourself with the Ramsar Convention guidelines on integrated planning process on URL: http://www.ramsar.org/pdf/lib/hbk4-02.pdf). Debate Ramsar guidelines on integrated planning approach.

4 Use the Ramsar guidelines to suggest improvements in the implementation of the Okavango Delta Management Plan.

5 What are some of the lessons from the case which can be used to inform future plans in other countries?

■   References

Ahn, B.Y., Lee, B.K. & Shafer, C.S. (2002) 'Operationalising sustainability in regional tourism planning: an application of the limits of acceptable change frame work', *Tourism Management*, **23**, 1-15.

Arntzen, J. (2005) 'Livelihoods, agriculture and biodiversity in the Okavango Delta, Botswana' report prepared for the PDF-B stage of the GEF project: 'Building local capacity for conservation and sustainable use of biodiversity in the Okavango Delta.

Atlhopheng, J. and Mulale, K. (2009) 'Natural Resource-based Tourism and Wildlife Policies in Botswana', in J. Saarinen, F. Becker, H. Manwa, & D. Wilson, (eds). *Sustainable Fourism in Southern Africa: Local communities and Natural Resources in Transition*, Bristol: Channelview Publications.

Barnes, T.J., Arntzen, J., Nherera, J., Lange, G. &Buzwani, B. (2006) *Economic Value of the Okavango Delta, Botswana and Implications for Management*, Gaborone, Botswana: World Conservation Union and the Government of Botswana.

Bramwell, B. & Lane, B. (1993) 'Sustainable tourism: an evolving of global approach? *Journal of Sustainable Tourism*, **1** (1), 1-5.

Chambers, R. & Conway, G. (1992) *Sustainable Rural Livelihoods: Practical Concepts for the 21st century*, Brighton: Institute of Development Studies.

Cooper, C., Fletcher, J., Fyall, A., Gilbert, D. & Wanhill, S. (2008) *Tourism, Principles and Practice*, Essex: Pearson Education Limited.

Darkoh, M.B.K. & Mbaiwa, J.E. (2009) 'Land-use and resource conflicts in the Okavango Delta, Botswana', *African Journal of Ecology*, **47**, 161–165.

Department of Environmental Affairs (2006) *Okavango Delta Ramsar Site Shared and Common Vision for 2016,* Gaborone: Department of Environmental Affairs and the World Conservation Union.

Department of Environmental Affairs (2008) *Okavango Delta Management Plan*, retrieved from http://www.mewt.gov.bw/DEA on 15 February 2013.

Farrell, B. & Twining-Ward, L. (2004) 'Reconceptualising tourism, *Annals of Tourism Research*, **32** (3), 274-295.

Farrell, B. & Twining-Ward, L. (2005). Seven steps towards sustainability: Tourism in the context of new knowledge. *Journal of Sustainable Tourism*, **13** (2), 109-122.

Grey, B. (1989) *Collaborating*, San Francisco: Jossey-Bass.

Innskeep, E. (1991) *Tourism Planning: an Integrated and Sustainable Development Approach*, New York: Van Norstrand Reinhold.

Jamal, T.B. & Getz, D. (1995) 'Collaboration theory and community tourism planning', *Annals of Tourism Research*, **22** (1), 186-204.

Kgathi, D.L., Mmopelwa, G., Mashabe, B. & Mosepele, K. (2012) 'Livestock predation, household adaptation and compensation policy: a case study of Shorobe Village in northern Botswana, Agrekon', *Agricultural Economics Research, Policy and Practice in Southern Africa*, **51**(2), 22-37.

Kgathi, D.L., Ngwenya, B.N. & Wilk, J. (2007) 'Shocks and rural livelihoods in the Okavango Delta, Botswana', *Development Southern Africa*, **24**(2), 289-308.

Kimbu, A.N. & Ngoasong, M.Z. (2013) 'Centralised decentralisation of tourism development: a network perspective', *Annals of Tourism Research*, **40**, 235-259.

Liu, Z. (2003) 'Sustainable tourism development: a critique', *Journal of Sustainable Tourism*, **16** (6), 459-475.

Magole, L. (2008) 'The feasibility of implementing an integrated management plan of the Okavango Delta, Botswana', *Physics and Chemistry of the Earth*, **33**, 906-912.

Manwa, H. (2011) 'Competitiveness of Southern African Development Community as a tourist destination', *Tourism Analysis*, **16**, 77-86.

Mbaiwa, J., Ngwenya, B.N. & Kgathi, D.L. (2008) 'Contending with unequal and privileged access to natural resources and land in the Okavango Delta, Botswana', *Singapore Journal of Tropical Geography*, **29**,155-172.

Mbaiwa, J.E. (2003) 'The socio-economic and environmental impacts of tourism development in the Okavango Delta, north-west Botswana', *Journal of Arid Environments*, **54**, 447-467.

Mbaiwa, J.E. (2005) 'The Problems and prospects of sustainable tourism development in the Okavango Delta, Botswana', *Journal of Sustainable Tourism*, **13**(3), 203-227.

Mfundisi, K.B. (2008) 'Overview of integrated management plan for the Okavango Delta Ramsar site, Botswana', *Wetlands*, **28** (2), 538-543.

Mill, R.C. & Morrison, A.M. (1998) *The Tourism System: An Introductory Text*, Iowa: Kendall/Hunt Publishing Company.

Government of Botswana (2003) *National Development Plan*, 9. Gaborone.

Pinheiro, I., Gabaake, G. & Heyns, P.(2003)'Cooperation in the Okavango River Basin: The OKACOM perspective', in A. Turton, , P. Ashton, & E. Cloete, (eds.), *Transboundary Rivers, Sovereignty and Development: Hydropolitical Drivers in the Okavango River Basin*, Pretoria: African Water Issues Research Unit/Green Cross International/University of Pretoria, pp. 105–118.

Ramsar (2013a) 'About the Ramsar Convention', retrieved from http://www.ramsar.org/cda/en/ramsar-about-about-ramsar/main/ramsar/1-36%5E7687_4000_0__ on 3 March 2013.

Ramsar (2013b) 'The Ramsar Convention and its mission', retrieved from http://www.ramsar.org/cda/en/ramsar-about-mission/main/ramsar/1-36-53_4000_0 on 3 March 2013.

Ramsar Convention (2013) 'Strategic Plan 2009-2015' retrieved from http://www.ramsar.org/pdf/strat-plan-2009-e-adj.pdf on 3 March 2013

Ramsar Secretariat (2013) 'The Ramsar Convention Manual', retrieved from http://www.ramsar.org/pdf/lib/manual6-2013-e.pdf on 3 March 2013

Ruhanen, L. (2008) 'Progressing the sustainability debate: A knowledge management approach to sustainable tourism planning', *Current Issues in Tourism*, **11** (5), 429-455.

Saarinen, J. (2006) 'Traditions of sustainability in tourism studies', *Annals of Tourism Research*, **33** (4), 1121-1140.

Sharpley, R. (2000). Tourism and sustainable development: Exploring the theoretical divide. *Journal of Sustainable Tourism*, **8**(1), 1-19.

Sheehan, L.R. & Ritchie, J.R.B. (2005) 'Destination stakeholders, exploring identity and salience, *Annals of Tourism Research*, **32** (3), 711-734.

Stankey, G.H., McCool, S.F. & Stokes, G.L. (1984) 'Limits of acceptable change: A new framework for managing the Bob Marshall Wilderness', *Western Wildlands,* **10**(3), 33-37.

Tao, T.C.H. & Wall, G. (2009) 'A Livelihood approach to sustainability', *Asia Pacific Journal of Tourism Research*, **14** (2), 137 - 152.

World Tourism Council (1997) *Sustainable Tourism Development: Guide for Local Planners*, Madrid: World Tourism Council.

World Travel and Tourism Council (2007) *Botswana: The Impact of Travel and Tourism on Jobs and the Economy*, London: WTTC.

■ Appendix: Vision and Goals of the Okavango Delta Management Plan

☐ Okavango Delta Vision

The common and shared vision for the Okavango Delta is: "A carefully managed, well-functioning ecosystem that equitably and sustainably provides benefits for local, national and international stakeholders".

☐ Overall Goal of the Okavango Delta Management Plan

The Overall Goal of the Okavango Delta Management Plan (ODMP) is: "to integrate resource management for the Okavango Delta that will ensure its long-term conservation and that will provide benefits for the present and future well-being of the people, through sustainable use of its natural resources"

☐   Strategic Goals and Strategic Objectives

Strategic Goal	Strategic Objectives
Institutional: To establish viable management infrastructure and tools to sustainably manage the delta resources at local, district, national and international levels.	To establish viable management institutions for the sustainable management of the Okavango Delta ecosystem To improve the regulatory framework for sustainable management of the Okavango Delta ecosystem. To raise public awareness, enhance knowledge and create a platform for information exchange and learning about the Okavango Delta ecosystem.
Biophysical: To ensure that the Okavango Delta and its associated dry lands continue to deliver present-day ecosystem services, and products for the benefit of all organisms dependent on it, including human beings.	To conserve the ecological character (biotic and abiotic functions) of the Okavango Delta, and the interactions between them. To maintain or restore the wetland habitats and ecosystems of the Okavango Delta.
Socio-economic: To sustainably use the Okavango Delta resources for improvement of livelihoods of all stakeholders that are directly or indirectly dependent on the ecosystem products and services of the Okavango Delta (and associated dry lands) in an equitable way.	To sustainably use the natural resources of the Okavango Delta in an equitable way and support the livelihoods of all stakeholders dependent on it. To sustainably use the wetland resources of the Okavango Delta for the long-term benefit of all stakeholders To develop socio-economic opportunities to improve livelihoods of the Okavango Delta stakeholders

3

4 Montenegro: Wild Beauty

Christian Baumgartner, *Naturefriends International*

Synopsis and Learning Outcomes

Despite tremendous pressures for rapid development of coastal tourism, mainly fuelled by foreign investment, the Ministry of Tourism together with its National Tourism Organisation (NTO) have "shifted the focus from traditional package tour holidays in coastal regions to creating a higher-yield tourism product based on nature tourism [and regional traditional culture]. This includes the promotion of local, authentic restaurants and hotel facilities, as well as the establishment of well-connected bicycle trails" (Montenegro National Tourism Organisation, 2010).

This case focuses on a 10-year development project in the region of the Biogradska Gora National Park in the north-eastern part of the country. A slow step-by-step development based on trust building, cooperation between five communities and the National Park and integration of regional stakeholders has resulted in sustainable tourism products that are successful in the international, mainly German-speaking market.

Naturefriends International (NFI) played an important role in the starting phase of the project in 1999 together with the country office of the OECD. Later on the tourism development project was financed by the Austrian Development Agency (ADA) and implemented by the ÖAR (Österreichische Arbeitsgemeinschaft für eigenständige Regionalentwicklung / Austrian Association for Endogenous Regional Development), while the author and NFI colleagues were continuously involved as experts, moderators or within monitoring processes.

The case of the development of the Bjelasica-Komovi region, with the central national park Biogradska Gora, shows that sustainable tourism development should have an eye on overall sustainable regional development, linking its specific products to regional resources and empowering regional stakeholders to gain benefit from the tourism development.

After completing this case study, learners should be able to demonstrate the following principles of sustainable tourism development:

1   The principle of participation of local and regional stakeholders to ensure the long-lasting success of the development.

2   The principle of local empowerment, especially in comparison with foreign investment.

3   The principle of systemic project management and step-by-step implementation plans.

■ Background

Montenegro (Crna Gora, meaning 'Black Mountain') was a part of former Yugoslavia. The country is situated with the Adriatic coast to the south-west and is bordered by Croatia to the west, Bosnia and Herzegovina to the north-west, Serbia to the north-east, Kosovo to the east and Albania to the south-east.

Montenegro has put in place several concrete measures in implementing the abstract ideas of sustainable development. In 2001 the Office for Sustainable Development was established. The same year, the Government adopted the first Masterplan for Sustainable Tourism Development. This plan clearly states that the responsibility for policy implementation lies with both an inter-ministerial committee and the private sector. In 2004 the 'Strategic Framework for Development of Sustainable Tourism in Northern and Central Montenegro' was adopted as the roadmap for development of the brand 'Wild Beauty' and, finally, the Parliament adopted the 'Tourism Development Strategy to 2020' in 2008.

There are 237,899 hectares under international protection and 100,000 hectares of pristine national parks, representing over 20 per cent of the country's 13,812 km² territory. In 1991 the Parliament articulated a bold vision, proclaiming Montenegro to be an Ecological State (National Tourism Organisation of Montenegro, 2010). Nature can therefore be understood as a logical resource for tourism development, especially in combination with the rich cultural landscapes of the hinterland.

The region of Bielasica-Komovi lies in the central north-east of the country and is characterised by its two mountain ranges: Bielasica – framing the Biogradska Gora National Park – and Komovi. The five municipalities of the region and the national park administrative body became partners in a 10-year development program that fosters active outdoor tourism, including hiking, rafting and mountain biking. The project has developed important linkages with the cultural assets of the region and created synergies with other economic sectors to generate regional benefit.

Some years after political will first enabled different development processes, the tourism outcomes have been largely positive. Destinations based on nature and culture have observed positive development of tourism related indicators. Tourist arrivals and overnight stays increased in the northern region between 2008 and 2010 in all months of the summer season (May till September). Hiking was the main activity in Montenegro for 67.1% of the questioned holidaymakers, followed by swimming (52.4%), enjoying good food (41.9%) and cultural sightseeing (41.3%).

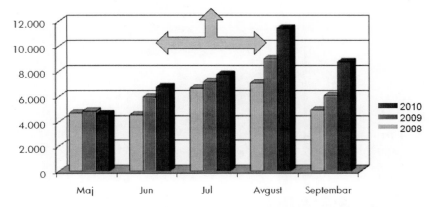

Figure 4.1: Number of tourists in the Northern Region (May-September 2008-2010).
Source: Monstat in: Montenegro Ministry of Sustainable Development and Tourism, 2011

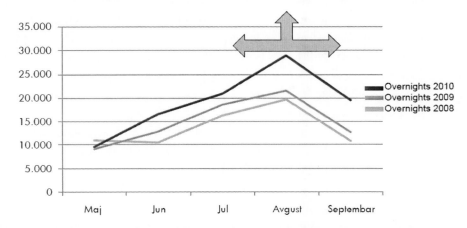

Figure 4.2: Number of overnights in the Northern Region (May-September 2008-2010).
Source: Monstat in: Montenegro Ministry of Sustainable Development and Tourism, 2011

According to figures from the Central Bank, total annual income from tourism has increased by 460% between 2001 and 2007, or from €86 million to €480 million (Montenegro Ministry of Tourism and Environment, 2008). In 2011, more than 1.5 million tourists visited Montenegro, with the Travel and Tourism economy representing 21% of the GDP (National Tourism Organisation of Montenegro, 2010). Despite these apparent gains, further improvements in tourism statistics and the development of a tourism satellite account system are necessary to be able to analyse results and trends in more detail.

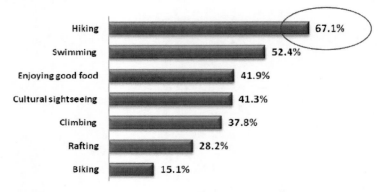

Figure 4.3: Main activities during the stay in Montenegro for tourists in the Northern Region. *Source:* Montenegro Ministry of Sustainable Development and Tourism, 2011

■ Key Concepts

The term 'sustainable tourism' has come to represent and encompass a set of principles, policy prescriptions, and management methods, which chart a path for tourism development such that a destination area's social and environmental resource base (including natural, built, and cultural features) is protected for future development (Lane, 1994). Sustainable tourism policies thus aim to balance the economic, social and environmental aspects of tourism development.

Sustainable development in tourism can be portrayed using a pentagonal pyramid (see Figure 4.4), with 'economic prosperity', 'intact nature', 'intact culture', 'well-being of the local population and the staff' and 'satisfaction of visitors' needs' at its base, while the top represents the inter-generational approach of sustainable development.

These concepts are aligned with other more general models of sustainable tourism in that they aim to show the linkages between economic, socio-cultural and environmental dimensions, which are focused on identifying solutions for the challenges of sustainability. However, this model shows the relationship between these aspects in a tourism context and the needs to balance the three pillars in safeguarding future developments at the tourism destination level, including the satisfaction of visitor needs. According to Baumgartner (2009), key aspects are:

■ Respect for the natural environment via public policies or private sector self-regulation;

- Embedding tourism in a sustainable, regionally-specific and networked fashion;

- Respect for the social well-being of the local population and the employees in the tourism-sector, as well as for the culture of the destination;

- Participation of the host community in the decision making and planning processes;

- The implementation of environmental management systems in intensely visited destinations; and

- Accountability of the public sector as the main stakeholder in maintaining the sustainability of tourism in the region.

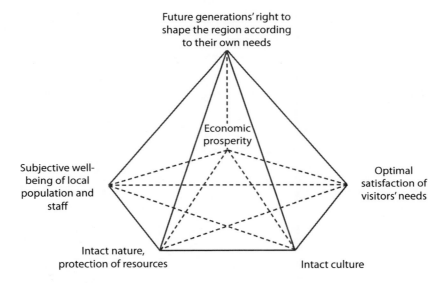

Figure 4.4: Müller (1999) adapted according to Baumgartner, 2009

Whilst this model seems simple, the reality of sustainable tourism develop-ment is more complex. These issues are compounded by the different levels at which sustainable tourism is implemented in the destinations. Planning and implementing sustainability measures at the destination level is a task that is often in the hands of or coordinated by the **local government**. This is also the level of government local residents are most likely to engage with in either opposing or supporting tourism development. In democratic political systems, local residents may expect to be able to influence or guide political decisions in this area, and have ways to voice their disagreements (Baumgartner, 2009). **Public participation** in sustainability planning at an early stage can avoid decisions being opposed by residents once they have been implemented. The content of planning processes could be improved and their implementation made more efficient if they were guided by public participation (Kollmann *et al.*, 2003).

The municipal level (i.e. cities and municipalities) is the lowest level in a democratic state system. In the everyday lives of most citizens, this is also where they come in direct and immediate contact with the 'state', 'public authorities', and thus with democracy. Therefore, the stability and acceptance of democratic political systems largely depends on how people experience democracy in a local context.

In practice, people often disagree or have difficulties and problems with the way political decisions are made in planning processes (Baumgartner, 2009). A top-down approach, presenting them with a *fait accompli*, leaves individual citizens no choice but to oppose it or put up resistance. However, if the population is empowered to get involved early on, the authorities and various experts can also learn from civil society and thus improve planning processes and find out much earlier how a given project will be received by the public. Public participation is therefore a key aspect of this case study.

Sustainable development and sustainable tourism can be seen as part of an integrated regional development process based on participation of all stakeholders. This principle entails several insights that should be taken into account in planning and management processes (Mose & Weixelbaumer, 2002):

- Interdisciplinary teamwork makes it possible to go beyond tourism and look at other economic sectors and/or areas of life as well.
- Planning and implementation of a given project needs to be preceded by integrated regional analyses involving the local stakeholders and communities.
- Planning and implementation must be accompanied by systemic project management.

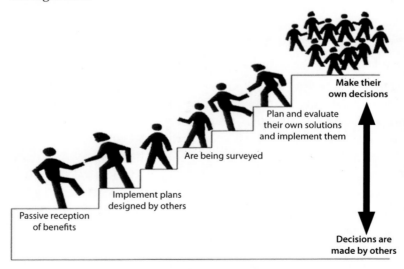

Figure 4.5: Participation Stages. *Source:* Steck *et al.*, 1999, based on GTZ-LISTRA-TÖB

■ Case Analysis

☐ Participation

The context for the development of this project was a country with a heavily centralised political system. With orders coming from the ministries in the capital, cooperation between municipalities, and especially between municipalities and national park administration and NGOs, was not common in Montenegro. There was no experience in regional development.

The project was based on series of workshops that followed different aims:

- Getting to know each other;
- Learning about sustainability;
- Learning the basics of sustainable tourism; and
- Discovering the interests of (international) tourists.

Participation has been one of the crucial elements of the project strategy in the Bjelasica region. Participatory processes can be rather time consuming and cannot always be planned in advance. In the beginning, the work was characterised by the following working tasks:

1 Identifying and establishing co-operations with representatives of the Ministry of Foreign Affairs located in Belgrade[1], representatives of the Bjelasica/Komovi region and international organisations working in Montenegro.

2 Collecting optional contacts and potential accommodation addresses relevant for the project (national parks and national park managements, leisure and education organisations, tour operators and guidebook publishing companies) and improving those contacts.

3 Organising a series of workshops. The aim was to strengthen the use of regional resources in a way that enables the established structures to work properly: Memorandum of Understanding, supporting local NGOs, building up project teams for the next project phases and realistic offers to other development projects.

Using a step-by-step approach, the workshop group developed a SWOT analysis of the region and formulated challenges for future development. One of the early visible results was the removal of car wrecks in the river bed which would impede the development of rafting tourism.

Another core target was the 'hidden agenda' of trust-building measures. It took the project team nearly two years to establish a Memorandum of Understanding (MoU), signed by all five mayors, ministers, the director of the National Park and an NGO representative. This MoU outlined common interests in the development

---

1   This was in the time before the status of Montenegro as independent state.

of the region, focusing on mountain tourism. It was followed by an Action Plan drafting and prioritising commonly discussed measures.

Peer-to-peer contacts with the Austrian Kalkalpen National Park and similar destinations were established. Visits of local stakeholders, e.g. to the Austrian Käsestrasse (Cheese Road) Bregenzerwald, showed comprehensive examples of regional development and the use of local agricultural products and handicrafts to create a regional selling point.

The national park involvement focused on two aspects: scientific background and environmental education. Nature trails and watchtowers formed not only attractions for tourists but also contributed to excursion programs for school classes.

The private botanical garden and the respective knowledge of a highly respected inhabitant of Kolasin was the nucleus for the later use of herbs to create local products for tourists. It was the first time that such local knowledge was actively looked for and citizens were included into decision-making processes.

It took quite a long time to reach agreement on key developments such as the location of the regional development office, and later the Regional Tourism Organisation (RTO). The local hiking associations analysed hiking trails and collaboratively determined the location for a new mountain hut. As a result, this decision was based on closing a gap along the hiking trails rather than arguing about which municipality deserved this infrastructure. These intensive discussion processes created acceptance and commitment for the development.

☐   Training and Professionalisation

Training and professionalisation were focussed on both the tourism hardware (e.g. accommodation and other infrastructure) and the software (e.g. services and activities). Based on the SWOT and a needs analysis, a training program for different stakeholders was developed and implemented – often in close cooperation with international experts. The Austrian Association of Alpine Organisations (VAVÖ) was responsible for the establishment of a mountain guide training program which fulfilled international quality criteria. Similar activities were developed for rafting and mountain biking. The training for the guides and the parallel-financed equipment enabled local associations to intensify their work with children and youth.

A part of the capacity building program was dedicated to the Montenegrin Mountain Rescue Service (GSS). New equipment was procured, exercises and knowledge tests were carried out for existing members and training for new members was offered. Finally GSS became a member of IKAR (International Mountain Rescue Organisation) to benefit from international contacts.

Locals were motivated and trained in running Bed & Breakfast establishments and insight into international tourism was gained by supporting tourism suppliers to attend international tourism fairs such as the Internationale Tourismus-Börse (ITB).

An important focus was put on ecological building construction. A new low-energy mountain hut, the new seat for the RTO as well as the watchtower in the national park were planned and constructed as exemplars. Internationally experienced architects and building companies cooperated with local craftsmen and used the construction sites for hands-on training.

Many tourism development projects financed by donor organisations 'forget' about marketing activities. In the case of Bjelasica, this was combined with capacity building for local agencies. A group of German speaking tour operators were invited for a combined familiarisation trip and workshop. They shared their experiences in the development of tour packages and services by local agencies that are needed for successful cooperation with foreign tour operators. As a result of such familiarisation trips and further promotion, Montenegro has won over 70 new specialised tour operators that offer nature and culture related packages on international markets. The majority of them (68%) are staying for 7-10 days within the country (National Tourism Organisation of Montenegro, 2010).

A further development stemming from the MoU and Action Plan was the 'Regional Tourism Strategy' which was presented in 2009 as one of the last activities of the Austrian-Montenegrin project partnership.

☐ Linkages to Regional Development

The project had a clear focus on a form of tourism that creates as much benefit for the local population as possible. Therefore, linkages to other sectors of the economy were an important project aim. Often local people were unable to imagine the interest of tourists in their 'everyday-products' such as herbs, berries or local varieties of fresh mountain cheese. But these local products contribute to regional distinctiveness and are an important foundation for marketing.

Existing initiatives were often identified and implemented by individual entrepreneurs. The first products that were sold in the new shop at the national park visitor centre were herbs, herbal teas and dried forest fruits. A working group developed quality criteria and a regional brand. But these initial developments also presented challenges, which provided important learning opportunities. The first tea packages were far too expensive as the group did not research prices in similar shops. Complaints from tourists resulted in more realistic prices. Soon handicrafts, wooden carvings and pottery complemented these tea packages. A new market for traditional handicrafts like weaving resulted in older residents passing on their skills to younger locals.

The region was lacking skilled tourism professionals for nearly all sectors. Education for cooks and waiters was rather poor in the whole of Montenegro. Existing tourism schools became local partners in an up-grading program that improved curricula, trained the teachers and invested in school equipment. In Kolasin, a traditional restaurant was linked with the kitchen of the tourism school. The students learnt how to cook and offered regional speciality weeks for locals and later also for tourists. This culinary offer brought renewed appreciation of the regional cuisine that was previously regarded as 'poor-people-meals'.

In summary, the 'tourism' development of Bjelasica-Komovi has created new jobs, rekindled traditions and contributed to local income for many families.

☐ Professional Project Management

The local project office employed a mixed team of international experts and locals – looking very carefully to qualifications but also to a regional distribution of jobs to avoid any distrust of the five municipalities. The creation of jobs and income brought early acceptance within the region.

Additional to the larger project modules which needed more time for implementation, a flexible small project fund was created to show quick results. Different initiatives such as waste collection activities in the mountains, reforestation, ski races for children, etc. could be carried out by private citizens or associations through this funding arrangement. Under-used activities to strengthen the sense of community were developed and eventually a large calendar of events was compiled.

An important target of the project was to establish sustainable outcomes which outlived the project period. The project partnership with the Austrian Development Agency was planned for 10 years, longer than usual in similar development projects. It created a stable structure, including the Regional Tourism Organisation which is financed and accepted by all five municipalities.

Several activities that were born within the small project fund were taken over by local associations as regular annual activities like the 'hiking opening' or the waste collection activities. Also the developed guide and mountain rescue trainings established regular structures that are linked with national or international umbrella organisations.

The project management used an intensive participatory approach to support the project development through public participation and involvement of relevant stakeholders with different methods within the phase of project implementation.

Table 4.1: Participatory approach within the timeline of the project

Project Step/ Task	Involved Target Group	Participation
Beginning of the project Information about the issue	Public (interested people, stakeholders from municipalities, national parks, alpine NGOs, tourism actors, local experts, entrepreneurs), governmental and donor-organisations, experts	Contribution: Concerned taking part in meetings and option to decide in small matters. Co-Discussion: Opinion is asked with rather little power of influence.
Memorandum of Understanding	Communities, governmental organisation	Co-decision and self-decision for community empowerment
Project proposal, presentation of the project and its targets, steps and milestones	Public (interested people, stakeholders from municipalities, national parks, hiking NGOs, tourism actors, local experts, entrepreneurs),	Co-Decision
Working on project tasks and outcomes, milestones	NGOs, communities, LTO and RTO	Contribution, co-discussion, co-decision
Small project fund, tourism offers, small local economic projects like collecting herbs for regional products	NGOs (hiking, mountaineering, rafting), local network of farming production	Self decision
End of the project	Local RTO and LTO together with tourism partners	Self administration

☐ Inclusion into National Frameworks

This regional development approach was not the only one taking place in Montenegro between 1990 and 2012. Different development cooperation organisations – mainly ADA (Austria) and GIZ (Germany), but also SNV (Netherlands), USAID (USA) and UNEP (United Nations Development Program) – put huge efforts into the sustainable tourism development of the country. To name a few projects:

- Wilderness Hiking and Biking Project in Northern Montenegro;
- Signposting and GIS registry of the long-distance hiking-trails Orjen-Lovćen-Rumija and Durmitor-Sinjavina-Bjelasica, setting the basis for links to European long-distance hiking-trails; and
- Tri-lateral national park development in the mountain range Procletije, together with the development of hiking infrastructure in Montenegro, Albania and Kosovo.

Several manuals for tourism suppliers, e.g. a hiking and biking manual, were published as well as series of new hiking and biking maps and guidebooks, e.g. *Wilderness Biking Montenegro* for tourists.

After the first Masterplan for Sustainable Tourism Development in 2001, the National Tourism Organisation (NTO) developed the brand 'Wild Beauty' creating a frame for all those nature related activities and including them into the national marketing strategies. In 2004, the Government adopted the 'Strategic Framework for Development of Sustainable Tourism in Northern and Central Montenegro' as the roadmap for development of 'Wild Beauty'. The 'Tourism Development Strategy to 2020', adopted in 2008, puts at least the same emphasis on 'Wild Beauty' offers and the sustainable tourism development of the mountain regions as on traditional beach and coastal tourism. This national recognition is crucial as it provides important backing for local and regional products to attract enough tourists to be sustainable.

■ Future Outlook

The tourism development in Bjelasica-Komovi is as satisfying as the development on a national level according to the quantitative and qualitative tourism indicators. Despite the economic crisis, Montenegro has experienced a strong increase in arrivals, overnight stays and income. The country has reached approximately 60% of the potential multipliers in Europe and in 2012, three to four 'early adopters' from North America began to prepare the first trans-continental packages.

Nevertheless, further development – both in terms of tourism and regional development in general – needs a deepening of the structural linkages between municipalities. The new Regional Tourism Organisation needs to be strengthened and protected against political changes at the local level. Continuous training measures should widen the sphere of benefits for the local inhabitants, develop new tourism products and improve the service quality.

A future-proof sustainable tourism policy for Montenegro as a country, after having set model regions and developed a political framework, needs to have:

- Implemented tools and criteria to monitor sustainability in tourism areas, as a basis for supporting and promoting specific regions in the future;
- Innovative programs to also improve the sustainability of coastal tourism;
- Institutional forms of communication between different political departments and local-regional-national levels with a mutual commitment to increasing and promoting sustainability;
- Marketing strategies with a special emphasis on existing sustainable approaches; and
- Complete integration of the topic of 'sustainability' into training and education in the tourism sector, and/or promotion and support of the corresponding approaches.

■ Summary and Conclusions

The case describes a 10-year development project in the region of the Biogradska Gora National Park in the north-eastern part of the country. Montenegro has shifted the focus from traditional package tour holidays in coastal regions to creating a higher-yield tourism product based on nature tourism. A slow step-by-step development based on trust building, cooperation between five communities and the National Park and participation of regional stakeholders has managed to develop sustainable tourism products that are successful in the international market. This participation and empowerment approach, guided by wise project management that balances regional benefits, has created commitment and stable structures that will continue after the end of the project period.

4

■ Study Questions

1 What are the relevant principles for sustainable tourism development in this case?

2 How important is participation for long-term success?

3 Compare tourism development in the Montenegrin hinterland (this case) with the development of coastal tourism (in Montenegro or in general) in terms of sustainability.

4 In terms of sustainable regional development, discuss how an empowerment approach may be more sustainable than foreign investment.

■ References

Baumgartner, C. (2009) *Nachhaltigkeit im Tourismus. Von der Tourismuspolitik für Nachhaltigkeit zu einem Bewertungsschema*, Innsbruck: Studienverlag.

Böll, H. (1977) *Einmischung erwünscht. Schriften zur Zeit 1973-1976*, Köln: Kiepenheuer und Witsch.

Kollmann G., Leuthold, M., Pfefferkorn W. & Schrefel, C. (Ed.) (2003) *Partizipation. Ein Reiseführer für Grenzüberschreitungen in Wissenschaft und Planung. Schriftenreihe Integrativer Tourismus und Entwicklung, Band 6.*, München / Wien: Profil Verlag.

Lane, B. (1994) 'Sustainable Rural Tourism strategies: A Tool for Development and Conservation', *Journal of Sustainable Tourism*, **2**, 102-111.

Montenegro Ministry of Tourism and Environment (2008) 'Montenegro Tourism Development Strategy to 2020', Podgorica.

Montenegro Ministry of Sustainable Development and Tourism, National Tourism Organisation of Montenegro (2011) 'Progress Monitoring – Wilderness Hiking & Biking Project Start 2008 – Results by 2010, with updates September 2011 For EcoTrophea 2011', Podgorica.

Mose, I. & Weixlbaumer, N. (2002) *Naturschutz: Grossschutzgebiete und Regionalentwicklung*, Sankt Augustin: Academia-Verlag.

Müller, H.R. & Flügel, M. (1999) *Tourismus und Ökologie: Wechselwirkungen und Handlungsfelder. Berner Studien zu Freizeit und Tourismus Nr. 37*, Bern: FIF Universität Bern.

National Tourism Organisation of Montenegro (2010) 'Country of Montenegro, Finalist, Destination Stewardship Award 2010', retrieved from http://www.tourismfortomorrow.com/Winners_and_Finalists/Previous_Winners_and_Finalists/2010_Winners_and_Finalists/country-of-montenegro/ on 28 December 2012.

Pollet-Kammerlander, D. & Asamer-Handler, M. (2008) 'Sustainable Tourism- and Regional Development in the North of Montenegro', Progress Report, Vienna.

Steck, B., Strasdas, W. & Gustedt, E. (1999) *Tourism in Technical Co-operation. A guide to the conception, planning, and implementation of project-accompanying measures in rural development and nature conservation*, Eschborn: GTZ.

5 Tourism and the Great Barrier Reef: Healthy Reef, Healthy Industry

Chris Briggs, *Great Barrier Reef Marine Park Authority*

Gianna Moscardo, *James Cook University*

Laurie Murphy, *James Cook University*

Margaret Gooch, *Great Barrier Reef Marine Park Authority*

Brian King, *Hong Kong Polytechnic University*

Synopsis and Learning Outcomes

The purpose of this case study is to highlight the key management strategies of the Great Barrier Reef Marine Park Authority (GBRMPA) to manage tourism in Australia's World Heritage Listed Great Barrier Reef (GBR). Recognised as one of the world's best managed coral reef ecosystems, the GBR is potentially better placed to handle the pressures of accumulating risks than many other reef systems. The GBR World Heritage Area extends to a vast 348,000km^2 and within this domain approximately 400 commercial tourism operators accommodate 1.8 million visitor days and 2.3 million passenger transfers each year. Established in 1975, the GBRMPA works within a strong legislative framework to manage the marine park and employs a range of regulatory tools and management plans to ensure that tourism is sustainably managed.

At the core of the GBRMPA approach is a recognition that tourism and the GBR are inextricably linked – a healthy reef equals a healthy tourism industry and vice versa. Stakeholder management and collaborative partnerships are regarded as central to the achievement of sustainable tourism on the GBR. These partnerships are based on the principle of mutual benefit and involve active engagement in decision making by a range of stakeholders. The stakeholder activities and programs that GBRMPA has employed have focused on capacity building, mutual learning, information generation and open communication. An Environmental Management Charge (EMC) is collected from visitors by tourism operators on behalf of the GBRMPA and contributes a substantial percentage of the annual budget for management of the Marine Park. However, the longer term outlook for the reef has deteriorated in the face of climate change, declining water quality (through runoff from catchments) and habitat losses associated with coastal developments. These challenges are compounded by increasingly constrained budgets and by the demands associated with managing multiple partnership programs (currently ten). In light of these circumstances, it will be important to maintain active and constructive communication with the tourism industry in order to foster stewardship and partnership.

After completing this case study learners should be able to:

1   Define the key collaborative concepts that apply to the management of relationships between tourism and environmental protection.

2   Identify the critical factors that contribute to the operation of effective partnerships for tourism in protected areas.

3   Outline the progress that has been made by the Great Barrier Reef Marine Park Authority since its establishment in balancing the needs of visitors and of the natural environment.

4   Explain how various partnership programs with stakeholders generally, and with the tourism sector in particular, can contribute to the maintenance of heritage values within a marine park setting.

5   Describe the actions that will be required to ensure a positive future for the Barrier Reef to the year 2050.

■ Background

Australia's Great Barrier Reef (GBR) is one of the most diverse natural ecosystems on Earth and is the world's largest coral reef system. The Great Barrier Reef World Heritage Area stretches 2,300 km along the Queensland coast, covers 348,000 km² and includes more than 900 islands. In 1981, it was inscribed on the World Heritage List in recognition of its outstanding natural values. The extraordinary variety of habitats and species in the GBR — many of them threatened — make it one of the world's richest and most complex natural ecosystems. Though similar habitats occur elsewhere, no other World Heritage Area contains such biodiversity. The area is of enormous scientific and intrinsic importance.

In 1975, the Australian Government established a statutory agency, the Great Barrier Reef Marine Park Authority (GBRMPA), to protect this natural treasure for the benefit of future generations. GBRMPA's authority is legislated through the Great Barrier Reef Marine Park Act 1975 and it reports to the Australian Government Minister for Sustainability, Environment, Water, Population and Communities. The GBRMPA's headquarters in Townsville employs approximately 200 full time staff working from Cape York to Fraser Island and in regional offices in Cairns, Mackay, Rockhampton and Canberra (see Figure 5.1). In managing and developing the Marine Park, GBRMPA's mission is to provide for long-term protection, for uses that are ecologically sustainable, and to facilitate understanding and enjoyment of the GBR on the part of all Australians and of the wider international community. The GBR is one of the world's best managed natural wonders attracting more than 1.6 million visitors annually, contributing more than AUD 5 billion to the Australian economy and generating 64,000 jobs. The Marine Park supports a variety of uses, particularly tourism, and is an integral part of the lifestyles and livelihoods of communities along the GBR coast.

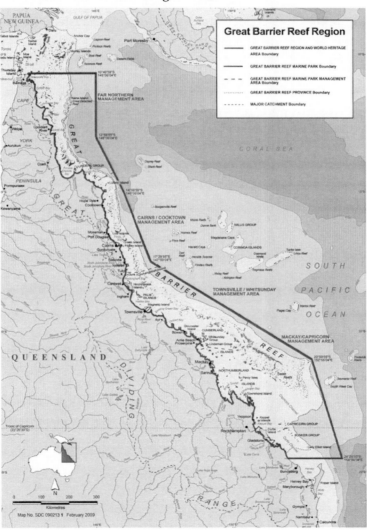

Figure 5.1: Great Barrier Reef Region

1920s	First Island Resorts Built
1940s	Begin using glass bottom boats to view coral reefs & first seaplane to Heron Island
1950s	Increased tourism infrastructure supports growth in tourism to the region
1960s	First underwater observatory built at Green Island
1970s	Game fishing captures celebrity attention & first live-aboard dive boats begin accessing more remote areas
1980s-90s	Rapid rise in tourism, especially from Asia & new boats allowing easier access

Figure 5.2: Brief History of Tourism Development on the Great Barrier Reef

Marine tourism in the GBR commenced around the turn of the 20th century with excursions to near shore reefs and islands. From these humble beginnings over a century ago, tourism has grown and now caters for approximately 1.8 million visitor days and 2.3 million passenger transfers annually. The timeline that is outlined in Figure 5.2 summarises the history of tourism to this iconic attraction. Today there are approximately 400 active tourism operators that operate across the Marine Park. Most operations are focused offshore from Cairns, Port Douglas and in the Whitsundays and these areas collectively account for about 80 per cent of tourism visitation to the Marine Park. The main opportunities available to visitors are nature-based and include; day vessel-based operations, floating pontoons, extended vessel charters, bareboat charters, cruise ships, aircraft-based operations and a myriad of shorter length activities such as parasailing. Marine tourism has become the region's largest reef-based industry and the GBR is central to an industry that generates AUD 5.1 billion each year and employs more than 64,000 people.

■ Key Concepts

The Great Barrier Reef is a major attraction for both international and Australian visitors. The marine tourism industry and the Reef are inextricably linked – a healthy tourism industry in the Great Barrier Reef Marine Park will always need a healthy Great Barrier Reef. Ensuring effective management of the GBR requires the support of a sustainable tourism industry. This **mutual interdependence** has led to a relationship between the GBRMPA and Marine Park tourism industry stakeholders. The **collaborative partnerships** that exist between the key **stakeholders** in tourism and the GBR are the core focus of this case study.

Table 5.1: Definitions of Key Concepts

Concept	Definition
Stakeholder	"any person, group, or organisation that is affected by the causes or consequences of an issue" (Bryson & Crosby, 1992)
Collaboration (in planning & management)	A process used by organisations that relies on joint decision-making about goals, strategies and practices needed to address problems amongst a group of relevant stakeholders (adapted from Jamal & Stronza, 2009).
Sustainable tourism	"Tourism that takes full account of its current and future economic, social and environmental impacts, addressing the needs of visitors, the industry, the environment and host communities" (United Nations World Tourism Organisation, n.d.)

According to Hall (1999), it is a truism that effective collaborative partnerships between stakeholders are a necessary component of sustainable tourism planning and management (see Table 5.1 for definitions of key concepts). The appropriateness of this approach has been acknowledged in the case of both tourism (de Araujo & Bramwell, 1999), and in protected area management (Caffyn & Jobbins, 2003). It is particularly important at the intersection between the two sectors (Kelly *et al.*, 2012). Three types of partnerships should be considered when connecting tourism and protected areas:

■ Those that facilitate the identification of problems associated with tourism and support the development of strategies towards sustainable tourism.

■ Those helping with the implementation of strategic practices that lead to more effective management of tourism and its impacts.

■ Those that enhance the role of tourism in supporting the broader goals of the protected area management agency (Jamal & Stronza, 2009; McCool, 2009).

This case will provide examples of all these types of partnerships between tourism stakeholders as they apply to the GBR.

Creating and maintaining effective stakeholder partnerships for tourism in protected areas is complex. The tourism phenomenon has direct impacts from tourist and operator actions at the site and indirect impacts from the actions of the broader tourism system. In the case of the GBR, the reef ecosystem can be affected by what tourists do at the reef and what they do elsewhere. This includes the coast adjacent to the GBR and overall impacts of tourism such as the carbon emissions associated with international travel (Moscardo, 2009). Tourism is a very diverse activity and overlaps with many other activities and phenomena. Tourists originate from throughout the world and may visit the GBR independently or with a smaller or larger tour operator. They engage in diverse activities using a variety of tourism businesses. Many different sectors and types of stakeholder are involved in GBR tourism. In many instances they are in competition with each other and with other users of the resource. The key stakeholders involved in GBR tourism are the protected area management agencies, tour operators active in the area, island resort owners and managers, communities that live in or adjacent to the GBR, conservation groups and tourists.

Although difficult and expensive to create, stakeholder partnerships are critical for the achievement of sustainable tourism on the GBR, and it is therefore important to understand the main factors that contribute to their effectiveness. A review of studies of collaborative stakeholder partnerships for tourism in protected areas has identified a number of critical factors for the implementation of effective partnerships. These included the following:

- An acknowledgement by all stakeholders of the mutual benefits of working together and the importance of the partnerships for achieving sustainable outcomes.

- Full and active engagement by all stakeholders in decision-making.

- A variety of partnership types that allow for involvement by a good representation of key stakeholders.

- Activities that help stakeholders to build capacity for participation in the decision making process and to implement the required practices.

- Processes that support mutual learning and that increase the information available for better management and planning decisions.

- Legislative and organisational support for the partnerships.

- Open communication and sharing of information.

(Sources: de Aruajo & Bramwell, 1999; Hall, 1999; Jamal & Stronza, 2009; Kelly *et al.*, 2012; McCool, 2009; Pfueller *et al.*, 2011; Wayers *et al.*, 2012; Waligo *et al.*, 2012).

■ Case Analysis

□ Overall Management Framework

The Great Barrier Reef Marine Park Act 1975 and Great Barrier Reef Marine Park Regulations 1983 provide direction for assessments of environmental impact and arrangements for tourism permits within the Marine Park. The use of spatial planning tools such as the Zoning Plan have established areas for nature-based tourism activities that are predominately free from potentially conflicting extractive uses. More detailed Plans of Management in the Cairns and Whitsunday areas have provided a range of visitor opportunities while managing key conservation issues and tourism growth. Visitor opportunities are created and maintained by managing a variety of 'settings' that define the size of vessels and permitted number of passengers, as well as the nature of activities permissible in specific settings. At the local level, supporting infrastructure such as moorings and reef protection markers which identify areas where anchoring is prohibited, may also assist in the protection of individual reefs, bays or islands. Marine Park tourists who visit the reef on a commercial vessel pay an Environmental Management Charge (EMC) which is collected by tourism operators on behalf of the GBRMPA. The EMC revenues generate approximately AUD 7 million each year and this is directed exclusively to Marine Park management and to in-park management, education and research. The revenues arising from EMC contributions can equate to as much as 20 per cent of the annual budget for Marine Park management.

The GBRMPA's detailed legislative and organisational framework has facilitated successful partnerships with reef tourism operators based on a common understanding of the need for a healthy reef to support healthy tourism. Tourism is the main conduit through which the GBRMPA fulfils one of its important international obligations - to present the Outstanding Universal Values of the Great Barrier Reef World Heritage Area to visitors. Table 5.2 provides a list of programs which underpins the strong partnership arrangements.

Table 5.2: Great Barrier Reef Tourism Partnership Programs

Program	Success Factors
Tourism & Recreation Reef Advisory Committee	Active engagement in decision-making Range of representatives
High Standard Tourism Program	Building stakeholder capacity Offering benefits for partners
Integrated Eye on the Reef Program Sightings Network Reef Health & Impact Surveys Eyes and Ears Incident Reporting Controlling Crown of Thorns Starfish	Mutual learning and better information for management Supports recognition of importance of partnerships Direct involvement in managing the GBR beyond just tourism impacts
Climate Change Adaptation & Mitigation	Active engagement in decision-making Building stakeholder capacity Offering benefits for partners
Responsible Reef Practices	Mutual learning and better information for management Offering benefits for partners
Reef Facts & Reef Discovery Course	Building stakeholder capacity Offering benefits for partners
National Landscapes Program	Offering benefits for partners

☐ The GBRMPA Tourism and Recreation Reef Advisory Committee

Since its establishment in 2000, the Tourism and Recreation Reef Advisory Committee (TRRAC) has played a critical role in developing the arrangements that are in place to manage tourism. This senior level, competency-based advisory committee comprises a cross-section of tourism and recreation stakeholders. The

TRRAC ensures that management arrangements, including policy and strategic directions, are developed in consultation with stakeholders and provides a platform to identify emerging tourism-related issues such as the effects of climate change on reef-based tourism. It also fosters indigenous participation in operating and managing tourism.

☐ High Standard Tourism Program

The GBRMPA provides tourism businesses with a range of benefits as an incentive to operate at a high standard both on land and within the Marine Park. An increasing number of marine tourism operators benefit from the environmental and marketing advantages of offering 'green' experiences together with the benefits provided by the GBRMPA such as 15-year permits (standard permit 6 years); showcasing at the annual Australian Tourism Exchange; promotion on the GBRMPA website; and referrals from visitor and media enquiries. In 2012, the program encompassed 60 operators and 123 individual tourism products, representing a steady rise since the scheme began in 2004. More than 65 per cent of tourists to the Great Barrier Reef now make use of high standard operators. To qualify, businesses must participate in Ecotourism Australia's ECO Certification program. This program involves an assessment of various areas, including business management and ethics, responsible marketing, customer satisfaction, environmental management and performance, climate action, interpretation and education, and cultural respect.

☐ Integrated Eye on the Reef Program

The Integrated Eye on the Reef program includes the Eye on the Reef Tourism Weekly Monitoring program, the Sightings Network and the Reef Health and Impact Survey programs. This long-running partnership between tourism operators, reef researchers and the GBRMPA provides a range of useful data and includes indicators of: reef health; the presence and abundance of iconic species; indicator and protected species; and unusual phenomenon. Over 30 operators regularly monitor more than 40 sites. The program provides long term data sets for researchers, acting as a warning system for outbreaks of crown-of-thorns starfish, and adds depth to information that is presented to reef visitors. This partnership arrangement is particularly successful in fostering reef stewardship.

☐ Sightings Network

The GBRMPA records and collates information about wildlife sightings provided by operators using a Sightings database. The Network is popular with operators and with researchers who may have an interest in a particular species, its distribution and behaviour. The database now incorporates in excess of 5,000 sighting reports and, for example, has been used to further our understanding of whales and their behaviour within the Marine Park.

☐ Reef Health and Impact Surveys

Increasing numbers of tourism operators have received training in assessing the impacts of extreme events such as cyclones, floods and coral bleaching using the GBRMPA's Reef Health and Impact Surveys. Operators are often best placed to reach sites promptly after an extreme event, undertake a survey, and convey their findings directly to the responsible parties.

☐ Eyes and Ears Incident Reporting

Since they are out on the water regularly, tourism operators are in a position to improve the effectiveness of the GBRMPA's compliance and enforcement measures by reporting any violations. Following advice from tourism operators, The Eyes and Ears incident reporting initiative was developed as an industry-specific reporting tool. It provides an effective method of detecting illegal activity and is a deterrent to illegal activities in areas of high tourism activity.

☐ Controlling Crown-of-Thorns Starfish

Early action by tourism operators in partnership with the GBRMPA can potentially reduce the severity of emerging outbreaks of crown-of-thorns starfish. Under a new AUD 1.43 million program announced by the Australian Government in June 2012, the peak marine tourism industry association, the Association of Marine Park Tourism Operators (AMPTO), is engaged in controlling crown-of-thorns starfish at high value tourism sites and undertaking broader population control measures.

☐ Climate Change Adaptation and Mitigation

Many Marine Park tourism operators are taking action to minimise their climate footprint, and to be 'business-ready' to adapt to a future shaped by climate change. The Great Barrier Reef Tourism Climate Change Action Strategy 2009–2012 has provided clear targets for the marine tourism industry and government to collaborate on tackling and adapting to climate change. The Climate Action certification scheme recognises operators who lead the way in adapting and mitigating the impacts of climate change. The scheme is now included in the standard assessment of Eco-Certified operations. The GBRMPA has also developed an emissions calculator targeted specifically at marine tourism enterprises with a view to helping operators understand the extent of carbon emitted by their operations and identifying potential reductions. There are now 140 registered users of this online

5

tool, which can help operators assess their emissions as part of gaining climate action certification with Ecotourism Australia.

☐ Responsible Reef Practices

A set of 31 environmental best practices, known as Responsible Reef Practices, were developed in partnership with the tourism industry and provide common sense guidelines about improving these activities to generate minimal impacts. The guidelines also provide information about minimum legislative requirements when operating within the Park.

☐ Reef Facts and Reef Discovery Course

A series of Great Barrier Reef Fact Sheets have been designed for tourism operators and their crew and provide accurate information about the values of the Great Barrier Reef World Heritage Area. These can then be conveyed to their clients. A Reef Discovery course is currently under development which will provide tourism staff with training in effective interpretative techniques and in reef and island ecology that can be shared with guests.

☐ National Landscapes Program

In March 2012, the Great Barrier Reef was designated as a National Landscape along with a prestigious group of Australian natural and cultural icons. The Australian National Landscapes program identifies landscapes which capture the essence of Australia and promotes these areas as distinct natural and cultural experiences for those with an interest in exploring the country. The program is a partnership between the Australian Government, conservationists and tourism operators. It aims to promote Australia's world-class, high-quality visitor experiences and to build support for the protection of Australia's natural and cultural assets. The program supports GBRMPA and tourism operators in promoting sustainable nature-based tourism experiences on the reef and its islands and ensuring that these experiences are protected into the future.

■ Future Outlook

The Great Barrier Reef is the world's largest and most diverse coral reef ecosystem, providing a wealth of visitor experiences including beachcombing, diving, whale watching, boating, fishing, and island resort stays. In 1981 it was inscribed on the World Heritage List in recognition of its unique attributes. It is recognised as one of the world's best managed coral reef ecosystems and is likely to survive the accumulating risks better than most other reef systems. Nevertheless, the

Great Barrier Reef Outlook Report 2009 identified that the current long-term outlook for the reef is poor and will be determined by decisions made over the next few years. Predicted climate change is dominating most aspects of the outlook into future decades. Other factors influencing the sombre outlook include a continued decline in water quality from catchment runoff and habitat loss associated with coastal developments.

One approach to reversing this negative trend is through strengthening the partnerships and stewardship arrangements that the GBRMPA has developed with the tourism industry. These aspects of management featured prominently in a recent strategic assessment by the Australian and Queensland Governments of the Great Barrier Reef World Heritage Area and adjacent coastal zone. The assessment resulted in an agreed, long-term sustainable development plan for the Great Barrier Reef Region. The plan provides greater certainty for industry and management decision-making, while ensuring the on-going protection of World Heritage values. The strategic assessment team assessed the capacity of existing management arrangements (including partnerships) to predict, monitor and report on multiple impacts and made recommendations for the improvement of current management approaches. The long-term future of the Great Barrier Reef will be influenced by decisions arising from the strategic assessment. However, the future outlook will depend substantially on the extent to which a global solution is found to climate change, the resilience of the reef ecosystem in the immediate future, and the quality and strength of partnerships with reef-based industries such as tourism.

An on-going challenge for the GBRMPA is maintaining the lines of communication with the tourism industry through TRRAC and other formal arrangements which foster stewardship and partnerships. Formal partnership arrangements have to be managed in the context of budget cuts, as there are fewer resources available to deal with the same management challenges; it is increasingly difficult for GBRMPA to engage in personal conversations with tourism operators and to maintain the necessary relationships for success. In future there will be greater reliance on the goodwill of peak industry bodies such as the Australian Marine Park Tourism Operators (AMPTO) – to play the role of reef champions.

■ Summary and Conclusion

Managing one of the world's most diverse natural ecosystems and largest coral reef systems is a challenging task. With a mission to provide for the long-term protection, ecologically sustainable use, and understanding and enjoyment of the GBR for all Australians and the international community, the GBRMPA has developed a range of collaborative stakeholder partnership programs with the tourism industry. At the core of these partnerships is the recognition of the importance of a mutually beneficial relationship – healthy reef = healthy tourism industry. The success of these programs will be crucial if the reef is to withstand future challenges. A commitment will be needed by the key stakeholders, as well as by GBRMPA, to engaged decision-making, to developing stakeholder capacity and to mutual learning. Improved management information will ensure the on-going success of the various programs and serve as a potential model for sustainable tourism management in other jurisdictions.

■ Study Questions

1   Though national parks have been around for over a century, the Great Barrier Reef Marine Park was one of the world's first marine parks. This case has highlighted the proactive leadership role of GBRMPA. How would you rate the progress that the Authority has achieved to date in balancing tourism development with environmental protection relative to the record of more recently established marine park authorities in other jurisdictions?

2   What are the different challenges associated with areas of the Marine Park where there is a high concentration of tourism related activity (eg. Cairns, Port Douglas and the Whitsundays) and less accessible and frequented areas?

3   Identify which of the challenges that are confronting the Marine Park to the year 2050 can be addressed through collective action by or with tourism industry operators and which challenges are less susceptible to their influence.

4   Whilst climate change looms as a particular medium to long term challenge, other unpredictable crises and emergencies may arise with little warning. These may or may not be associated with climate change. Suggest a crisis type situation that might arise in the Marine Park and how a concerted response might help to remedy the situation with particular reference to any tourism-related implications. What roles would you attribute to the relevant public authorities and to tourism operators in this scenario? Prepare an evaluative report which summarises what occurred, the remedies that were adopted and the extent to which the problem was mitigated.

■   References

Bryson, J.M. & Crosby, B.C. (1992) *Leadership for the Common Good: Tackling Public Problems in a Shared-Power World*, San Francisco: Jossey-Bass.

Caffyn, A. & Jobbins, G. (2003) 'Governance capacity and stakeholder interactions in the development and management of coastal tourism: Examples from Morocco and Tunisia', *Journal of Sustainable Tourism,* **11** (2&3), 224-245.

de Araujo, L.M. & Bramwell, B. (1999) 'Stakeholder assessment and collaborative tourism planning: The case of Brazil's Costa Dourada project', *Journal of Sustainable Tourism,* **7** (3&4), 356-378.

Deloitte Access Economics Pty Ltd (unpublished) 'Economic Contribution of the Great Barrier Reef', report prepared for the Great Barrier Reef Marine Park Authority, December 2012.

Hall, C.M. (1999) 'Rethinking collaboration and partnerships: A public policy perspective', *Journal of Sustainable Tourism,* **7**(3&4), 274-289.

Jamal, T. & Stronza, A. (2009) 'Collaboration theory and tourism practice in protected areas: Stakeholders, structuring and sustainability', *Journal of Sustainable Tourism,* **17**(2), 169-189.

Kelly, C., Essex, S., & Glegg, G. (2012) 'Reflective practice for marine planning: A case study of marine nature-based tourism partnerships', *Marine Policy,* **36**, 769-781.

McCool, S.F. (2009) 'Constructing partnerships for protected area tourism planning in an area of change and messiness', *Journal of Sustainable Tourism,* **17**(2), 133-148.

Moscardo, G. (2009) 'Challenges for tourism development and management on Australia's Great Barrier Reef Coast', in R. Dowling & C. Pforr (eds.), *Coastal Tourism Development,* New York: Cognizant Communication, pp. 252-264.

Pfueller, S. L., Lee, D., & Laing, J. (2011). Tourism partnerships in protected areas: exploring contributions to sustainability, *Environmental Management,* **48**(4), 734-749.

Skeat, A. and Skeat, H. (2007) 'Tourism on the Great Barrier Reef: a partnership approach', in R. Bushell and P.F.J. Eagles (eds.) *Tourism and Protected Areas - Benefits Beyond Boundaries,* Wallingford, United Kingdom: CAB International, pp. 315-328.

United Nations World Tourism Organisation (nd). 'Sustainable development of tourism: Definition', retrieved from http://sdt.unwto.org/en/content/about-us-5 on 9 December 2012.

White, L. & King, B.E.M. (2009) 'The Great Barrier Reef Marine Park: Natural Wonder and World Heritage Area', in W. Frost & C.M. Hall (eds.), *Tourism and National Parks: International Perspectives on Development, Histories and Change,* London: Routledge, pp. 114-127.

Waayers, D., Lee, D., & Newsome, D. (2012). Exploring the nature of stakeholder collaboration: a case study of marine turtle tourism in the Ningaloo region, Western Australia, *Current Issues in Tourism,* **15**(7), 673-692.

5

Waligo, V. M., Clarke, J., & Hawkins, R. (2012). Implementing sustainable tourism: A multi-stakeholder involvement management framework, *Tourism Management*, **36**, 342-353.

INTERNATIONAL CASES IN SUSTAINABLE TRAVEL & TOURISM

6 Leading the Way: Accor Standing for Children's Rights in Tourism

Camelia Tepelus, *End Child Exploitation and Trafficking, USA*

Synopsis and Learning Outcomes

Accor, one of the leading global hotel operators represented in 90 countries all over the world, is a corporate leader on tourism sustainability. While the responsible operations of Accor cover a wide range of aspects, the purpose of this case study is to focus on the issue of protecting children from trafficking and sexual exploitation within the overall sustainability strategy of Accor. The company has a long history of engaging on child protection, being the first global corporation to formally join a voluntary Code of Conduct in 2002 and operating consistently at the forefront of the advocacy agenda on social responsibility in tourism.

The objective of the case study is to document Accor's work on child protection over the last decade, explaining the corporate philosophy behind it and its theoretical fundaments and presenting the practices implemented into the company's operations. This is done by highlighting a variety of instruments and measures that Accor has put in practice and the impacts they have had in strengthening the corporate brand and partnerships with a variety of stakeholders.

The main finding of the case study is that despite addressing one of the most challenging and highly sensitive topics within the tourism sustainability agenda, Accor has successfully identified appropriate internal and external communication procedures and expertise sources, allowing the company to become a pioneer, then a leading voice championing the protection of children's rights as an integral component of the contemporary tourism sustainability agenda.

The case study draws from stakeholder theory and modern strategic social responsibility research, showing how Accor's work with a wide range of stakeholders has allowed the company to innovate within a sustainable tourism niche that is less often addressed by large companies.

Upon completing the case study, learners will achieve an understanding of the challenges related to issues of child protection in tourism, and be able to explain:

1   The risks that trafficking and sexual exploitation of children pose to a tourism company.

2   The factors that should be taken into account when creating a company-wide strategy to prevent sexual exploitation and trafficking.

3   How a company can engage with a sensitive and potentially negative phenomenon in a way that will positively contribute to building its corporate sustainability brand.

■ Background

☐ Company structure

With more than 3,500 hotels in 92 countries, Accor is one of the world's leading hotel operators. Its brand portfolio ranges from luxury to budget including brands in all categories: Sofitel (luxury), Pullman and MGallery (upscale), Novotel and Mercure (midscale), ibis, ibis Styles, ibis Budget, hotelF1. Accor identifies itself as the only hotel group active across all hospitality market segments. At the end of 2012, the Accor network portfolio was located: 31% in France, 30% in Europe (other than France), 1% in North America, 23% in Asia Pacific, 8% in Latin America and Caribbean and 6% in Africa and the Middle East (see Figure 6.1 below).

Accor worldwide   3,516 HOTELS | 450,487 ROOMS | 92 COUNTRIES

North America
17 hotels
4,998 rooms

France
1,515 hotels
137,567 rooms

Europe (excl. France)
1,038 hotels
139,443 rooms

Latin America and Caribbean
226 hotels
35,330 rooms

Africa and Middle-East
166 hotels
28,355 rooms

Asia Pacific
554 hotels
104,794 rooms

Figure 6.1: Accor distribution of brands and properties, by geographic region (Figures at 31 December 2012)

The 2012 financial results indicate consolidated revenue of € 5,649 million and market capitalisation valued at € 6.7 billion. 63% of the revenue generated in 2012 was from upscale and midscale brands, 35% from economy and 1% from other businesses.

The company was founded in 1967 and is headquartered in Paris, France. As of the end of 2012, the Accor shareholding was: 75.9 % in floating shares and 24.1% in shares owned by board members and founders.

Accor created its first Environmental Department in 1994, which merged into the Sustainable Development Department in 2003 (Tourism for Tomorrow Awards, 2010). In 2006, the 'Earth Guest' program was launched, mobilising Accor's 145,000 employees, millions of customers and thousands of suppliers and partners. Earth Guest consolidates a range of existing sustainability projects around eight priorities divided into two broad-based themes:

1 *EGO projects:* focusing on support for local development, child protection, fighting epidemics, promoting healthy eating and balanced food.

2 *ECO projects:* which aim to reduce water and energy consumption, improve waste sorting and recycling programs and preserve global biodiversity.

Accor aims to integrate these eight sustainable development priorities at each stage of a hotel's life and with all stakeholders.

Also in 2011, Accor launched a sustainability research program which published the report '*Sustainable Hospitality: ready to check in?*' in June of that year. The survey questioned 6,973 hotel guests in six countries, for all hotel types (chains, independent hotels, etc) and segments (budget to luxury). The six countries surveyed were: Australia, Brazil, China, France, Germany and the United Kingdom. The selection was made in order to allow comparisons between countries of different cultures, with varying levels of economic development; mature and emerging. The research revealed child protection to be one of the four key areas where hotel guests had high expectations for concrete actions from the company.

☐ Legal Context

The link between protection of children from sexual exploitation and trafficking, on one hand, and sustainable tourism practices, on the other hand, is not immediately apparent without explaining the legal context of the phenomenon. Globalisation has increased demand for cheap labour and fomented a worldwide human trafficking industry estimated at USD 9 billion in annual profits, for which 600,000 to 800,000 people are trafficked across international borders every year (Glover, 2006). Many of them are children and teenagers from impoverished rural communities migrating to large urban areas or tourism destinations in search of work opportunities, but vulnerable to labour or sex exploitation.

While adult sex tourism is better known in traditional tourism research circles (Carter and Clift, 2000; Garrick, 2005, etc), child sex tourism and trafficking are niche topics which only started to receive attention in the 70s and 80s. O'Connell Davidson and Sanchez Taylor (1995) carried out important field research on child sex tourism in the 90s in Thailand, India, Venezuela, the Dominican Republic, South Africa and Cuba. Their reports, commissioned by the advocacy network ECPAT International (End Child Prostitution, Pornography and Trafficking), informed the proceedings of the 1996 1st World Congress against the Commercial Sexual Exploitation of Children, where for the first time governments committed to combat sexual exploitation of children recognised it as an international crime, including in tourism. It is important to note that adult prostitution is legal and a legitimate economic activity in some countries, consequently adult sex tourism, while controversial, is not a crime when it involves consenting individuals over 18 years old. However, tourism for the purpose of sexual relations with a minor is a 'clear and unambiguous violation of human rights' (UNWTO, 2004), being criminalised under national and international legislation. A tourist who engages in sex with a minor commits a violation of several international conventions, notably of the UN Convention of the Rights of the Child and of the Optional Protocol on the Sale of Children, Child Prostitution and Child Pornography, as well as of further applicable child protective national legislation in a particular country jurisdiction.

In the last couple of years, legal developments have turned child sex tourism into one of the indicators calling attention to the larger phenomenon of trafficking in human beings, "the 21st century form of the old worldwide slave trade" according to the UN Office on Drugs and Crime (UNODC, 2006). Human trafficking is defined by UNODC in the context of the UN Convention against Transnational Organised Crime and two of its supplementing protocols: the Protocol to Prevent, Suppress and Punish Trafficking in Persons, Especially Women and Children and the Protocol against the Smuggling of Migrants by Land, Sea and Air, both adopted by the UN General Assembly in 2000. Trafficking in human beings is defined by UNODC (2006) as:

> the recruitment, transportation, transfer, harbouring or receipt of persons, by means of the threat or use of force or tougher forms of coercion, of abduction, of fraud, or deception, or the abuse of power or of a position of vulnerability or of the giving or receiving of payments or benefits to achieve the consent of a person having control over another person, for the purpose of exploitation. Exploitation includes, at a minimum, the exploitation of the prostitution of others or other forms of sexual exploitation, forced labour or services, slavery or practices similar to slavery, servitude or the removal of organs.

It is the aspects of "transportation, transfer, harbouring or receipt of persons" in the trafficking definition that make it possible for tourism businesses to be used, voluntarily or involuntarily, in relation to trafficking in human beings.

The links between trafficking and child sex tourism are also noted by the US Department of State Office to Monitor and Combat Trafficking in Persons (TIP Office), which issues an annual Trafficking in Persons Report (TIP Report). The TIP Office lists other governments' efforts to combat child sex tourism amongst the measures to eliminate trafficking in persons. The Protection Project at John Hopkins University (Protection Project, 2007) reviewed the 2006 edition of the TIP report, finding that 29 countries were referenced as either origin or destination countries for child sex tourism. In regard to minor victims of sex tourism and trafficking, the legal determination is clear: "children under 18 cannot give valid consent, and any recruitment, transportation, transfer, harbouring or receipt of children for the purpose of exploitation is a form of trafficking regardless of the means used" (UNHCHR, 2000).

UNICEF quotes surveys indicating that 30 to 35 per cent of all sex workers in the Mekong sub-region of South East Asia are between 12 and 17 years of age, 2 million children are believed to be exploited through prostitution and pornography, and 1.2 million children are trafficked every year (UNICEF, 2007). While child sex tourism is booming worldwide, according to Glover (2006) Asia is at the centre of child prostitution, with 60,000 child prostitutes in the Philippines, 400,000 in India and 800,000 in Thailand. Most of them are girls under the age of 16, or boys in the case of Sri Lanka's 20,000 child prostitutes. A common misconception is that sex tourists are primarily paedophiles (Tepelus, 2008). However, the majority of perpetrators are primarily prostitute users in general, without a pathological preference for minors (Glover, 2006). Children are sought in the most impoverished areas to be brought to developed entertainment destinations, often tourism destinations, to serve the red light districts. Criminal sex traffickers recruit victims from rural areas, often crossing national borders to neighbouring villages where children do not to speak the native languages. Often the parents are told that children would become domestic servants, waiters or cleaners. Instead, the children are forced into prostitution or into other forms of exploitative work (begging, pick-pocketing, small thefts, etc.), often in tourist destinations.

☐ The Work of Accor on Child Protection in Tourism

At the centre of the Accor commitment to child protection is its early engagement with the Code of Conduct for the Protection of Children from Sexual Exploitation in Travel and Tourism, (The Code, www.thecode.org). In 2002, Accor was the first large company to sign The Code. The Code is a voluntary, self-regulatory mechanism for the travel industry, developed by the non-governmental network ECPAT (End Child Prostitution and Trafficking) and advised by UNICEF and UN World Tourism Organisation. The Code signatory companies commit to implement into their operations six basic steps:

- Establishing ethical corporate policies rejecting the sexual exploitation of children.

- Periodically training personnel in the country of origin and in destinations.

- Introducing clauses in contracts with suppliers calling for the repudiation of sexual exploitation of children.

- Providing information to travellers through a variety of channels (catalogues, ticket-slips, posters, websites, etc.).

- Establishing contact with 'key persons' in destinations.

- Annual reporting on implementation (Tepelus, 2004).

Since its start in 1998, funding of The Code has been from public sources including the European Union (1999-2004), UNICEF (2004-2011) and currently the Swiss Government, with a small contribution from private sector memberships.

In 2002, Accor started to incorporate the protection of children from sexual exploitation into its sustainability strategies, initially for its Asia operations. After an initial pilot stage, following high interest and positive feedback from stakeholders (notably employees, civil society and management), the expansion of child protection policies continued across different organisational brands. Currently, The Code is signed by Accor operations in 36 countries: Thailand, Cambodia, Laos, Indonesia, New-Zealand, Fiji, Hungary, Romania, Russia, Germany, Austria, France, Switzerland, Netherlands, Poland (Orbis), Benin, Cameroun, Cote d'Ivoire, Ghana, Guinea Conakry, Equatorial Guinea, Nigeria, Senegal, South Africa, Chad, Togo, Madagascar, Dominican Republic, Brazil, Argentina, Chile, Colombia, Ecuador, Peru, Uruguay, Mexico.

The main outcomes of this process include extensive staff training, guest awareness and many other complementary awareness raising initiatives and fundraising. Over the last 5 years, the Accor group has trained over 70,000 employees to combat sexual tourism involving children, enabling staff to recognise situations in which children are at risk and to respond immediately.

Regarding guest awareness, most hotels in the countries that have signed The Code inform their customers of Accor's commitment by relaying ECPAT campaigns (films, flyers, posters and publicising other communication tools) (see Figure 6.2).

In addition to implementing the Code of Conduct, the company supports the child protection cause in other ways, notably through direct fundraising for ECPAT and public campaigning. In Asia, Accor regularly organises fund raising actions to benefit ECPAT educational projects. In 2009, for Earth Guest day, Accor Thailand employees organised a large bowling tournament. Through the ticket sales and prizes for the winners, Accor collected funds for ECPAT and children centres run by YMCA, which serve children who were victims of sexual exploitation. Similar examples of good practices include training sessions in Morocco, where educational sessions were given to managers and employees on how to identify and combat child sex tourism. All staff in Marrakech, Agadir and Casablanca attended multiple awareness raising sessions organised by the Accor Human Resources department in partnership with the Morocco non-profit organisation Acting for Life. In Brazil, the Accor Academy created a kit in order to train hotel managers to fight against child sex tourism. More than 4,600 Accor Brazil employees were trained in 2009. The hotels also received flyers in order to sensitise their guests.

Figure 6.2: Samples of Accor sponsored awareness raising materials for the hotels to share their commitment with their guests by displaying posters and flyers. From left to right, samples from 2002 (France) to 2003-2011 (Thailand) and 2012 (Poland).

■ Key Concepts

Accor's commitment to children's rights in an international context is backed theoretically by **stakeholder theory** (Clarkson, 1995) which argues that companies have a **social responsibility** requiring them to consider the interests of all parties affected, or potentially affected, by their actions. Stakeholders include not only the parties in direct fiduciary relationships with the company – shareholders, management, suppliers, employees, creditors (primary stakeholders) – but also the parties potentially impacted by the operations of the company – local communities, the environment and the society as such (secondary stakeholders) (Jacobs, 1997). The core of normative stakeholder theory as developed in the 1980s and 1990s is that freedom is best served by seeing business and **ethics** as connected (Freeman *et al.*, 2004) leading to what is desirable for the society.

A more recent interpretation on the stakeholder theory takes into consideration the strategic development priorities of the corporation. From this perspective, **corporate social responsibility** should be considered as a form of **strategic investment** (Porter and Kramer, 2006; McWilliams *et al.*, 2006), and consequently treated as all investment decisions are treated. The case for corporate responsibility is supported in this view by four main arguments which all call for a strategic approach: moral obligation, sustainability, license to operate and reputation.

Accor's engagement in children's rights protection on an international scale is supported by Porter and Kramer's (2006) classification of the social issues faced by a company into the categories of:

- *Generic:* important to society but not immediately relevant to the company's long-term competitiveness.

- *Value chain social issues:* significantly affected by the company's ordinary activities within its value chain.

- *Issues from the competitive context:* factors in the external environment affecting competitiveness in places the company operates.

The early adoption of child protection policies and training practices fulfils Porter and Kramer's recommendation for companies to prioritise and focus on the **value chain** and strategic CSR practices. The long-term engagement with the non-profit advocacy ECPAT over the course of more than a decade confirms the deep conviction within Accor that child protection needs to become a critical generic societal issue. This is reflected in the statement "as guests of the Earth, we welcome the world", which expresses the very core of Accor philosophy based on hospitality and respect for diverse cultures.

Furthermore, strategies integrating social responsibility practices in the core operations of the company require extensive institutional processes within the overall strategy, operations and policies. In this context, it is significant to note that Accor's first formal and public signing of the ECPAT Code of Conduct took place in 2002, correlating with the launch of the Sustainable Department in 2003, from which child protection activities have continued to expand.

However, it is also important to have in mind that such integration of a potentially sensitive issue within a wider sustainability strategy comes not only with advantages, but also with exposure to potential risks:

- Possibility of negative public reactions including susceptibility and criticism.

- Negative public image, or creating negative connotations for tourism destinations.

- Criticism, rejection and unfair treatment from local and national authorities that may be concerned of political and social implications of the topic.

It is not uncommon for governments or local authorities to be rather concerned that **stewardship** on child protection from a business operating in tourism destinations would not attract positive feedback, but rather negative attention. In this regard, it is important to note that making the 'business case' for a tourism company to engage in child protection may be perceived as a difficult task. Unlike the case of the environmental components of tourism sustainability (i.e. resource conservation, biodiversity protection, water and energy savings) where the cost savings constitute the main rationale, child protection may not pay off immediately, if at all.

Making the business case for social issues in general remains a topic still vividly debated in corporate citizenship research. Studies of the association between responsible corporate ethics and profitability indicate that often the two go together, however, a causal link is still far from being fully proven. A comprehensive study conducted by Orlitzky *et al.* (2003) as a meta-analysis of 52 other studies integrating 30 years of research shows that corporate virtue in the form of CSR and, to a lesser extent, environmental sustainability 'is likely' to pay off. Orlitzky *et al.* find "a positive association between corporate social and financial performance across industries". Importantly, they also find that "market forces do not penalise companies that are high in corporate social performance; thus managers can afford to be socially responsible".

Case Analysis

6

Considering the sheer scale and depth of Accor's impact on the protection of children from sexual exploitation, its global leadership in the field is widely recognised. There are two key elements that have allowed Accor to become one of the leading corporate pioneers on tourism sustainability and child protection: first, implementation of a continuous and rigorous performance measurement system and second, a comprehensive approach to sustainability and viewing children's rights not as a separate element, but as an integral part of its corporate responsibility strategy.

Regarding the metrics, performance management and monitoring processes, the overall numbers speak for themselves. Between 2006 and 2011, 70,000 employees were trained to identify cases of sex tourism involving children and to react appropriately and in 2012, 30,000 additional employees were trained. In 2008, over 11,700 employees were part of the program, and in 2009, 13,000 were trained in Asia and sub-Saharan African countries to detect suspicious behaviours and know how to react, thanks to a global procedure containing all necessary information. Accor properties in 36 countries have signed the ECPAT Code of Conduct. Accor estimates that 49% of all its properties had formally committed to child protection by 2011, while the target for 2015 is set at 70% (Accor, 2013). The strategic approach of implementing child protection policies followed a geographic progression that started with Asia, then gradually expanded to Latin America, sub-Saharan Africa, Russia and Eastern Europe. The overall group objective is to continue spreading Accor's commitment country by country within the group (especially in Europe and Asia),'in-bound' a well as 'outbound' destinations, by strengthening staff training programs and customer awareness. According to the most recent information from Accor as of March 2012, Accor's commitment to children's rights within P21 is being broadened beyond the fight against sexual exploitation to the protection of children in general, notably by relaying national missing children alerts in Accor hotels (AMBER alerts) and facilitating reintegration and sustainable life projects for marginalised minors. AMBER alerts are law enforcement programs set by governments to pursue and solve cases of child abduction, including training of teams to watch out and be part of the reaction chains. In 2011, 66 Accor hotels have initiated programs to help marginalised minors reintegrate into society. In Thailand for example, Accor supports the UNICEF 'Youth Career Development Program' aiming to provide Thai girls and boys aged 17 to 20 with 5 months' practical and theoretical training in the hotel industry.

It is significant to note that the company developed suitable metrics and performance indicators not only for child protection but also opened itself for public scrutiny of its overall sustainability strategy. Accor has been a participant in the UN Global Compact since 2003, periodically providing sustainability reports according to the international guidelines. Accor has been listed since 2004 in four of the most recognised international benchmark indexes: the Dow Jones Sustainability Index, the FTSE4Good, the Aspi Eurozone and the Ethibel Sustainability Index. The Accor leadership on tourism sustainability is probably best demonstrated by the company receiving in 2011 the 'SAM Silver Class' distinction from SAM, one of the leading sustainability investment analysis companies. The Silver Class is for companies that received a score within a range of 1% to 5% from the score of the Sector Leader. Table 6.1 below shows the quantification on Accor consistently outperforming between 2006 and 2011 its peers in the tourism sector.

Table 6.1: Results of Accor rating in the SAM classification

Year	Accor Rating	Sector Average
2011	77%	52%
2010	78%	56%
2009	84%	56%
2008	70%	42%
2007	66%	37%
2006	68%	43%

However, as demonstrated by the WTTC Global Tourism Business Award 2010, probably the most important feature of the Accor child protection program is its seamless embedding within the wider group sustainability strategy, which involves a holistic set of aspects: environmental, community, cultural and social.

These were not included in the scope of this case study which focused mostly on child protection. These work areas are structured under the umbrella designated as PLANET 21, a reference to Agenda 21, the action plan adopted by 173 Heads of State at the 1992 Earth Summit in Rio de Janeiro. This also reflects on the Accor commitment to play its role in the change of production and consumption patterns. Figure 6.3 presents the 21 indicators of the Accor PLANET 21 program.

7 pillars	21 commitments	21 quantifiable objectives for 2015
Health	1. Ensure healthy interiors	**85%** of hotels use eco-labeled products
	2. Promote responsible eating	**80%** of hotels promote balanced dishes
	3. Prevent diseases	**95%** of hotels organize disease prevention training for employees
Nature	4. Reduce our water use	**15%** reduction in water use between 2011 and 2015 (owned/leased hotels)
	5. Expand waste recycling	**85%** of hotels recycle their waste
	6. Protect biodiversity	**60%** of hotels participate in the Plant for the Planet reforestation project
Carbon	7. Reduce our energy use	**10%** reduction in energy use between 2011 and 2015 (owned/leased hotels)
	8. Reduce our CO_2 emissions	**10%** reduction in CO_2 emissions between 2011 and 2015 (owned/leased hotels)
	9. Increase the use of renewable energy	**10%** of hotels use renewable energy
Innovation	10. Encourage eco-design	**40%** of hotels have at least three eco-designed room components
	11. Promote sustainable building	**21** new or renovated hotels are certified as sustainable buildings
	12. Introduce sustainable offers and technologies	**20%** of owned and leased hotels offer green meeting solutions
Local	13. Protect children from abuse	**70%** of hotels have committed to protecting children
	14. Support responsible purchasing practices	**70%** of hotels purchase and promote products originating in their host country
	15. Protect ecosystems	**100%** of hotels ban endangered seafood species from restaurant menus
Employment	16. Support employee growth and skills	**75%** of hotel managers are promoted from internal mobility
	17. Make diversity an asset	Women account for **35%** of hotel managers (outside Motel 6 / Studio 6)
	18. Improve quality of worklife	**100%** of host countries organize an employee opinion survey every two years
Dialogue	19. Conduct our business openly and transparently	Accor is included in **6** internationally-recognized socially responsible investment indices or standards
	20. Engage our franchised and managed hotels	**40%** of all hotels are ISO14001 or EarthCheck certified (excl. economy segment)
	21. Share our commitment with suppliers	**100%** of purchasing contracts are in compliance with our Procurement Charter 21

Figure 6.3: Accor PLANET 21 program including its 7 pillars, commitments and quantifiable objectives for 2015

The comprehensiveness of Accor's sustainability work in its entirety has been widely acknowledged and awarded at the international level with distinctions including: 'Tommorrow's Value Rating' (2009), Voyages-sncf Responsible Tourism Award' (2008), 'Grand Prix AXA Santé' Award (2008), Condé Nast Traveler's World Savers Awards (2009), World Travel&Tourism Council 'Tourism for Tomorrow Award' (2010), IFTM TOP RESA trade show's 'Lauriers du Voyage d'Affaires' (2010), Sustainable Development Gold Scepres (2010) and Global Vision Awards (2010) from the 'Travel+Leisure' magazine. Specifically for the Accor global policy to fight sexual exploitation and trafficking of children in tourism, Accor received in 2011 the Condé Nast Traveler's World Savers Award.

■ Future Outlook

The extensive experience developed on child protection in the context of sustainable tourism development unquestionably makes Accor a pioneer and a steward in the field of sustainability and human rights in tourism. Although the sheer scale of the company's expansion makes implementation of its child protection program an on-going challenge in itself, several other areas remain to be further developed. These include:

- Outreach of the program to properties in destinations with specific legislative or political challenges – such as the USA or China.
- Continuous development and internal management of the monitoring process.
- Refining internal protocols and external communication strategies to raise public and peer awareness of the issue of child protection in the context of tourism.
- Balancing the company's work on child protection within the wider sustainability strategy of the group.

■ Summary and Conclusion

This case study presents the framework and operational processes of the Accor group, a leading global hotel operator committed to protecting children's rights to live free from sexual exploitation and trafficking, in the context of sustainable tourism development.

Accor's collaborative, multi-stakeholder approach to a topic of such sensitivity is an example for the sector. The company embarked in early 2002 on a long-standing campaign backed by coherent programmatic action to incorporate the issue of child protection within its sustainable development philosophy, whose application over the last decade was rewarded in 2010 with a WTCC Global Tourism Business Award. Accor's holistic and multi-faceted engagement with sustainability, including one of the most difficult and publicly sensitive topics, demonstrates that tourism businesses can successfully and effectively raise societal expectations, becoming agents of change towards a more sustainable 21st century society.

■ Study Questions

1   What political and social factors should a company take into consideration when approaching the development of its social sustainability strategy?

2   In what context should a company assess its risk and exposure to sexual exploitation and trafficking of children?

3   Discuss, compare and contrast the child sex tourism vulnerability of destinations in Western Europe the Caribbean and South East Asia?

4   Analyse issues regarding media reports on trafficking or sexual exploitation of children in your region, and make recommendations for the tourism private sector.

■ References

Accor (2011) 'Sustainable Hospitality: ready to check in? A world premiere: the first international tracking study on hotel guest expectations regarding sustainable development' retrieved from http://www.accor.com/fileadmin/user_upload/Contenus_Accor/Developpement_Durable/img/earth_guest_research/dossier_de_presse_eng_bd.pdf on January 28, 2013.

Accor (2012) 'Accor in brief', retrieved from http://www.accor.com/fileadmin/user_upload/Contenus_Accor/Franchise_Management/Documents_utiles/General_information/accor_en_bref_uk.pdf on 28 January 2013.

Accor (2013) 'The seven pillars of Planet 21. Local', retrieved from www.accor.com/en/sustainable-development/the-7-pillars-of-planet-21/local.html on 28 January 2013.

Carter, S. & Clift, S. (2000) 'Tourism, international travel and sex: themes and research', in S. Clift, and S. Carter (eds.), *Tourism and Sex: Culture, Commerce and Coercion*, London: Pinter.

Clarkson, M.B.E. (1995) 'A stakeholder framework for analyzing and evaluating corporate social performance', *Academy of Management Review*, **20** (1), 92-117.

Costa Rica, Cuba, Dominican Republic, Venezuela, South Africa, Thailand, series of papers undertaken for ECPAT International as preparation for the World Congress Against the Commercial Sexual Exploitation of Children, retrieved from www.ecpat.net/eng/Ecpat_inter/projects/sex_tourism/sex_tourism.asp on 15 June 2007.

Freeman, E.R., Wicks, A.C. & Parmar, B. (2004) 'Stakeholder theory and "The corporate objective revisited"', *Organisation Science,* **15** (3), 364 – 369.

6

Garrick, D. (2005) 'Excuses, excuses: Rationalizations of Western sex tourists in Thailand', *Current Issues in Tourism*, 8 (6), 497-509.

Glover, K. (2006) 'Human trafficking and the sex tourism industry', *Crime & Justice International*, **22** (92), 4-10.

Jacobs, M. (1997) 'The environment as a stakeholder', *Business Strategy Review*, **6** (2), 25-28.

McWilliams, A., Siegel, D. & Wright, P. M. (2006) 'Corporate social responsibility: Strategic implications', *Journal of Management Studies*, **43** (1), 1-18.

O'Connell Davidson, J. & Sanchez Taylor J. (1995) 'Child prostitution and sex tourism in Goa'. *Research Paper*. Bangkok: End Child Prostitution in Asian Tourism.

Orlitzky, M., Schmidt. F.L. & Rynes, S.L. (2003) 'Corporate social and financial performance: A meta-analysis', *Organisation Studies*, **24** (3), 403-441.

Porter, M.E. & Kramer, M.R. (2006) 'Strategy and society: The link between competitive advantage and corporate social responsibility', *Harvard Business Review*, December 2006, 78-94.

Protection Project (2007) *International Child Sex Tourism. Scope of the Problem and Comparative Case Studies*. Washington D.C.: The Protection Project at the Johns Hopkins University, Paul H. Nitze School of Advanced International Studies.

Tepelus, C. (2008) 'Social responsibility and innovation on trafficking and child sex tourism: Morphing of practice into sustainable tourism policies?', *Tourism and Hospitality Research*, **8** (2), 98-115.

Tepelus, C. (ed.) (2004) Code of Conduct to Protect Children from Sexual Exploitation in Travel and Tourism. Overview and Implementation Examples, Madrid: UNWTO.

Tourism for Tomorrow Awards (2010). Application Form, Accor.

UNHCHR (2000) 'Protocol to Prevent, Suppress and Punish Trafficking in Persons Especially Women and Children, supplementing the United Nations Convention against Transnational Organised Crime. Art 3c.', retrieved from http://www2.ohchr.org/english/law/protocoltraffic.htm on 28 January 2013.

UNICEF (2007) 'Child protection from violence, exploitation and abuse. The big picture. Issues addressed under child protection', retrieved from http://www.unicef.org/protection/index_bigpicture.html. UNICEF on 15 June 2007.

UNODC (2006) *Trafficking in Persons: Global Patterns*, Vienna: UNODC.

UNWTO (2004) *Indicators of Sustainable Development for Tourism Destinations. A Guidebook*, Madrid: UNWTO.

7 Banyan Tree: Embracing the Environment, Empowering People

Tanya MacLaurin, *University of Guelph*

Michael Chiam Kah Min, *Ngee Ann Polytechnic*

Synopsis and Leaning Outcomes

Banyan Tree Hotels and Resorts (commonly known as 'Banyan Tree') is a subsidiary of Banyan Tree Holdings Limited which has its global headquarters in Singapore. Since the inception of Banyan Tree in 1992, the company has received many prestigious awards and accolades for its leadership in sustainable practices. One of these awards was received in 2012 from the World Travel and Tourism Council (WTTC) recognising Banyan Tree as a pioneer in sustainable tourism development. Banyan Tree state that, "while we are honoured to receive these awards, they remain to us rewards not incentives." Founded on the core value of driving sustainable development, the company seeks to be an agent of social and economic development through responsible tourism. Environmental conservation is a top priority in the development of the company's resorts. Banyan Tree has boutique hotels, resorts, and spas across six continents. This case presents information on the environmental initiatives implemented at the first integrated resort in Asia, Laguna Phuket, under the visionary guidance of their Co-founder and Executive Chairman, Mr Ho Kwon-Ping.

The purpose of the case study is to provide a platform for developing an understanding of entrepreneurial strategic sustainable development in the hotel industry. The concepts of *entrepreneurship, core values, sustainability, corporate social responsibility* and *corporate shared value* are demonstrated by Banyan Tree's development of Laguna Phuket in Bang

Tao Bay, Thailand. The issue of environmentally ravaged land being developed into an exemplary model of sustainable tourism development is demonstrated in the case. Best practices developed at this first initiative can be seen as impacting future developments and the daily operations of all Banyan Tree properties.

After exploring this case study learners should be able to:

1   Define entrepreneurship and discuss its role in the sustainable development at Bang Tao Bay.

2   List and explain sustainable practices taken by Banyan Tree at the micro, meso and macro levels of the Laguna Phuket development at Bang Tao Bay.

3   Discuss the relationship of Banyan Tree's core values with their co-founders, Mr Ho Kwon-Ping and Ms Claire Chiang.

4   Describe the role of strategic sustainable development decision making at the Bang Tao Bay development.

5   List best practices developed at Laguna Phuket and discuss how they have impacted future Banyan Tree developments.

6   Define corporate social responsibility and corporate shared value. Discuss their impact on Banyan Tree's sustainable development policies, procedures and daily operations at their properties.

■ Background

Mr Ho Kwon-Ping (commonly known as 'KP Ho') is the Executive Chairman of the Thai Wah/Wah Chang Group. He took over the reins of the company after his father had a stroke in 1981. KP's values and leadership directed the company toward their future in sustainable development (Laguna Phuket, 2013). In the initial years of the Group's operations, its main business was in trading commodities such as starch and vermicelli, food production, as well as property development and construction. Initially, the Group enjoyed a significant cost advantage over its competitors; however, with the passage of time, the competition became far more challenging. The Group decided to look for other growth opportunities and consequently this led the company to acquire a piece of land in Bang Tao Bay, Phuket, Thailand in the 1980s. This purchase started their journey into the hospitality industry.

As the Group's business in the hospitality industry grew, it established Banyan Tree Holdings Limited in 1992. Subsequently, Banyan Tree Holding Limited expanded its business to establish and to manage other hotels, resorts, and related businesses. The company was registered in Singapore with KP Ho as Executive Chairman; his wife, Claire Chung, as Senior Vice President (Retail); and his brother, Ho Kwon Cjan, as the head architect of the company.

Banyan Tree Hotels and Resorts (commonly known as 'Banyan Tree') is a subsidiary of Banyan Tree Holdings Limited and owns two brands, 'Banyan Tree' and 'Angsana'. While the 'Banyan Tree' brand is targeted at affluent travellers looking for classic experiences in romance, intimacy and rejuvenation, the 'Angsanas' brand, launched in 2000, is designed for more contemporary experiences and revitalisation.

Both brands operate boutique hotels, resorts, and spas across six continents, which stretch from as far north as Ireland to the Australian cities of Sydney and Cairns in the south and from as far west as South Africa to China and Japan in the East. In total, Banyan Tree owns 29 hotels and resorts, 65 spas and 81 galleries, as well as two golf courses. Its 9,000 associates come from 27 countries (see Figure 7.1). Banyan Tree hotels, resorts and spas are often located in or near environmentally sensitive locations around the world, where they are caring for the environment and seeking to be positively contributing members within the host communities. With a motto of "Embracing the Environment, Empowering People", Banyan Tree pursues sustainability through the three pillars of enhancing operational efficiencies, building local capacity and conserving biodiversity.

Figure 7.1: Banyan Tree Properties, 2011. *Source:* Banyan Tree (2012)

☐ First Development

In 1983, a 1000-acre plot of land in Bang Tao Bay, Phuket, Thailand, was acquired by the Thai Wah Resorts Development Public Company Limited of Bangkok, a subsidiary of the Thai Wah/Wah Chang Group, to develop into a resort (see Figure 7.2) (Banyan Tree, 2013a). However, the Group faced a considerable challenge as this piece of land was severely ravaged as it had previously been used for tin-mining. At the time of the acquisition, the land was described by KP Ho as: "Much of the land looked as though it had just gone through war, totally denuded, piles of blackened soil, craters in the ground, broken huts and rusting piles of discarded machinery, here and there. The tin-mining had really torn everything apart."

Figure 7.2: Bang Tao Bay before Development

The past activities to dredge for tin led to removal of trees and vegetation, which in turn led to topsoil erosion. The leaching of chemicals used in tin mining and the presence of difficult soil such as sand and marine clays made the land completely inhospitable to natural life. In fact, unbeknownst to the Thai Wah/Wah Chang Group, the United Nations Development Plan (UNDP) team had described the land as devoid of any potential for tourism development back in 1977. In 1979, the Tourism Authority of Thailand (TAT) also wrote the site off as "highly polluted due to in-land mining activities." Nonetheless, the company persevered to restore the land and turn it into a hospitable environment for natural life.

Starting from scratch, the Group led by their Executive Chairman, KP Ho, brought in experts to advise on the restoration process. First, the tortured contours of the site were smoothed out; the contours had been destroyed by years of extensive dredging. Then fresh topsoil was imported to the site. The Group sought to preserve the remaining trees in its design of roads and buildings, as and when it was possible. Native trees and plants that had been destroyed by the tin mining process were replanted en masse to restore the lush tropical vegetation that had covered the site before tin mining commenced.

The land was eventually restored and the Laguna Phuket — the first integrated resort in Asia — came into being (see Figure 7.3) (Banyan Tree, 2013a). The whole investment cost 5,000 million baht (US$200 million), the largest single investment in Phuket. The resort comprises seven hotels, namely Dusit Thani Laguna Phuket, Laguna Beach Resort, Angsana Laguna Phuket, Banyan Tree Phuket (the flagship hotel of Banyan Tree), Best Western Allamanda Phuket, Laguna Holiday Club Phuket Resort and Outrigger Laguna Phuket Resort and Villas. In addition, it houses an 18-hole golf course known as Laguna Phuket Golf Club, Canal Village Shopping Centre, Quest Laguna Phuket Adventure, the Chapel-On-The-Lagoon wedding chapel, and numerous residential neighbourhood developments (Laguna Phuket, 2013).

Figure 7.3: Bang Tao Bay and the Laguna Phuket

Since developing Laguna Phuket, the company has added other hotels to its list in different parts of the world which are managed under the 'Banyan Tree' and 'Angsana' brands. For its effort in environmental conservation and their excellent business model, Banyan Tree has won many prestigious awards and accolades including 'American Express and International Hotel Association Environment Awards' in 1992, 'Best Hotel Bangkok' in 2011 and was one of four winners of the 'World Travel & Tourism Council's Tourism for Tomorrow Award' in 2012. Also in 2012, Mr. KP Ho was awarded CNBC's Travel Business Leader Award in the Asia Pacific region. The award recognised Mr. Ho as a business pioneer demonstrating leadership excellence in innovation and management skills who was paving the way forward in a dynamic sector.

■ Key Concepts

☐ Entrepreneurship

During a speech at the Global Entrepreneur Summit in 2006, Ms Claire Chiang, KP's wife and co-founder of Banyan Tree, talked about the role of an **entrepreneur** as a factor of success at Bang Tao Bay. According to the model developed by McMullen and Shepherd (2006), an entrepreneur must first understand or possess an understanding of the natural and communal environment before he can recognise sustainable development opportunities. If an entrepreneur's knowledge of the threat to the natural/communal environment is high, it is more likely that he or she will recognise the opportunity for sustainable development. Subsequently, Patzelt and Shepherd (2010) expanded the model to incorporate three additional factors: the motivation of the entrepreneur; the perception of threat to the natural/communal environment; and altruism. Altruism is the focus of care and concern for the welfare of others. In other words, if the entrepreneur's knowledge of the threat to the natural/communal environment is high, he or she may not only recognise the opportunity for sustainable development but also be motivated to improve the welfare of those living within the community (altruism). When KP Ho wanted to develop Bang Tao Bay into Laguna Phuket, an integrated resort, he saw the need to do it differently from the usual focus on the profitability of the business venture. Beyond making a profit for his business venture, KP Ho sought to be a responsible developer: he also wanted to preserve the environment. For him, the preservation of both the physical and human environment was vital. Therefore, Mr Ho was motivated and determined to remediate the wasteland purchased in Bang Tao Bay. The restoration process included hiring environmentalists and other experts, along with the restoration of topsoil with fertiliser, despite incurring enormous costs.

Mr Ho first displayed his understanding of the negative impact of business development on the natural environment in his speech at the 1992 International Hotel Association Environment Award Gala Dinner: "The global tourism industry has both the potential to destroy through insensitive development, the very source of existence, or to create a symbiotic relationship with our natural environment, preserving and enhancing it for future generations to enjoy." KP Ho also shared his interpretation of the concept of 'environment' as having two dimensions: the physical environment and the human environment. This concept became Banyan Tree's motto 'Embracing the Environment, Empowering People'.

Apart from restoring the land, Mr Ho decided not to destroy the trees at the property in Laguna Phuket; instead, roads and buildings had to be designed around these trees. Today, Banyan Tree has a policy of planting native species which both represent the local ecology and do not require heavy maintenance to survive and thrive.

☐ Core Values

Core values are traits, qualities, and guiding principles that represent an individual's or organisation's highest priorities. Core values are deeply held and are fundamental driving forces. Core values define what an organisation believes and provides the foundation for all business activities (Heathfield, 2013). The core values of Executive Chairman Mr Ho Kwon-Ping shaped the core values of Banyan Tree's sustainable development at Bang Tao Bay, the future site of Laguna Phuket. Indeed, Banyan Tree was founded on the core value of driving sustainable development. This core value is pursued via the three pillars of enhancing operational efficiencies, building local capacity and conserving biodiversity. Banyan Tree's triple bottom line of economic, social and environmental success directs sustainable development by aiming to inspire associates, guests and partners to take a wider consideration encompassing a long-term view when making business and consumption decisions.

The definition of sustainable development was published in 1987 by the United Nations in a report commonly referred to as the *Brundtland Report*, *Our Common Future*. Sustainable development was defined as "development which meets the needs of the present without compromising the ability of future generations to meet their own needs". "The theoretical framework for sustainable development evolved between 1972 and 1992 through a series of international conferences and initiatives" (United Nations, 2010). In 1992, the principles of sustainable development were established at the United Nations conference on Environment and Development in Rio de Janeiro, Brazil (United Nations, 2010).

☐ Corporate Social Responsibility and Shared Value

The concept of **corporate social responsibility** has evolved, since its inception in the 1950s, to encompass the ways in which a company manages its economic, social and environmental impacts, with a focus not only on what a company does with its profits but also on how they make them (Levy and Duverger, 2010; Harvard Kennedy School, 2008; Porter and Kramer, 2006; Carroll, 1999).

In 2001, Banyan Tree further formalised its corporate social responsibility efforts with the creation of the Green Imperative Fund (Banyan Tree, 2013b). The fund is a mechanism to provide funds for externally focused social and environmental efforts, thus widening the reach and effectiveness of the company's efforts to provide critical financial support to worthy environment action and community based projects where Banyan Tree Holdings has a presence. Banyan Tree is also a creator of shared value as described by Porter and Kramer (2011) as a concept creating economic value in a way that also creates value for society by addressing its needs and challenges.

Many of Banyan Tree's programs focus on preserving marine life. One of them is the fish stocking policy for all its lagoons in Laguna Phuket. This is to restore eco-balance in the lagoons within their properties. Another program is the preservation of turtles which are found in locations like the Maldives, Binta and the Seychelles (see Figure 7.4). During the annual breeding season of sea turtles, Banyan Tree cordons off the resort's beach to provide a safe area for the turtles to lay their eggs. Besides having programs that aim to preserve marine life, they also have other programs that try to preserve land-based endangered species such as elephants and other wildlife.

Figure 7.4: Sea Turtles at Laguna Phuket

Banyan Tree considers itself to be a change agent in the social and economic development of the communities in which it operates. Its staff dormitories resemble the guest accommodation of three-star hotels. The company also operates the Thai

Ministry of Education certified Laguna Phuket Kindergarten for the benefit of its employees and provides space for residents based upon specific needs. Finally, the hotels have purchased handicrafts from villages around Thailand for their hotel rooms and public spaces.

The knowledge and experiences the company has acquired from its properties in Laguna Phuket have been replicated in its other properties or businesses around the world. Specifically, Banyan Tree has sought to uphold the following core values: 1) preservation of the environment; and 2) the enhancement of the lives of its employees and the communities in which it operates.

■ Case Analysis

Banyan Tree Hotels & Resorts has been conscientious in its endeavour to preserve the human and physical environment of all its properties around the world. Its conservation efforts are enshrined in the following core values that have ensured consistency across all its properties (Banyan Tree, 2011):

- Provide our associates with fair and dignified employment to enhance their ability to contribute to the company's growth in the long term, while improving their job prospects at Banyan Tree and beyond.

- Promote the long-term societal prosperity of the communities in which we operate via our business conduct and operations, while harnessing our key competencies to address issues facing the community.

- Exercise caution and care in order to limit the environmental impact of our operations and play an active role in the protection and the remediation of our global ecosystem.

These core values underpin Banyan Tree's policies and business practices, some of which follow. The discussion of these policies and practices will be divided along the lines of the company's key concerns: physical environment (environmental projects and environment resource conservation) and human environment (local communities).

□ Physical Environment: 'Embracing the Environment'

Environmental Projects

In order to safeguard the environment around the properties in which it operates, Banyan Tree has developed environment preservation initiatives to educate its associates, guests and the local communities. For instance, at its properties in Sanya and Phuket, Banyan Tree organises regular beach cleaning activities which involve guests, associates and locals. The purpose is to highlight the importance of keeping the beaches clean as well as to minimise the adverse long-term impact of the pollution of the sea, which affects the lives of marine creatures. Angsana Velavaru in the Maldives organises a monthly reef cleaning dive, involving many of its guests. Since the launch of this activity in 2007, a total of 4,406 coral predators such as the 'crown of thorns' starfish have been removed to better protect the reefs.

Many properties such as those in Bintan, the Maldives, Phuket, and Mayakoba have sought to educate their guests about the importance and purpose of environmental conservation through conservation presentations. Banyan Tree invites their guests to participate in complimentary activities such as guided nature walks, guided tree trail walks and bird watching trips. Besides targeting adults, properties such as Banyan Tree Phuket have also provided daily programs for children under 10. The objective of these programs is to engage the children's five senses through the exploration and appreciation of the natural environment.

Banyan Tree Gallery in Thailand launched the exclusive Elephant Collection to commemorate Thai Elephant Day that is held annually on 13 March. Besides selling the Elephant Collection, the gallery also organises photo exhibitions in Bangkok and Phuket to showcase the Elephant Nature Foundation and its advocacy of the welfare of Asian Elephants in Thailand. Proceeds from the sale of the photographs and limited edition Elephant T-shirts, as well as 5% of Banyan Tree Gallery's total revenue from 13 March to 13 June are donated to the Elephant Nature Foundation.

Banyan Tree Hotels and Resorts have also set up two conservation laboratories in Bintan and the Maldives to study the conservation of turtles, marine life, coral, and the rainforest. For instance, the Maldives Lab studies the diet of fin fish so as to safeguard the vital food chains supporting marine biodiversity and fisheries. In addition, it also collaborates with Banyan Tree Vabbinfaru to conduct regular marine conservation presentations to educate people about turtle conservation and monitor coral bleaching. This process enables the researchers to determine which species of coral will survive best in the warmer water. These species of corals could be used to create a new reef in the water around the Banyan Tree's properties (see Figure 7.5).

The Banyan Tree Bintan Conservation Lab conducted coral planting with guests to celebrate Earth Day in 2011. It has worked with Reefcheck to support the organisation in the preservation of Indonesia's coral reefs. Furthermore, the Lab has also collected turtle eggs and hatched them; the baby turtles are then released into the sea. Guests are invited to witness the turtle release and attend educational talks on the conservation of turtles. The Lab also maps and monitors its coastal rainforest ecosystem; monitored species include birds, snakes, coral and sea turtles.

Figure 7.5: Barnacle Reef Regeneration

Environment Resource Conservation

Since 2007, Banyan Tree has launched a group-wide effort to monitor and systematically reduce the energy consumption, water consumption and water production at each resort. It set up a subsidiary, Banyan Tree's GPS Development Services (GPS), to conduct environmental studies at its properties. Some of the completed projects are:

■ *Replacing gasoline engines with electric motors in pontoon ferries.* Pontoon ferries are used to ferry guests from Banyan Tree Phuket to the other hotels in Laguna Phuket. GPS conducted a three-month study on the environmental impact of the four-stroke gasoline engines used in the pontoon ferries. Once the gasoline engines were found to have a negative impact on the environment, they were replaced with electric motors that afford cleaner propulsion than the traditional gasoline engines, though their costs of operation are higher.

■ *Installation of solar panels on buggies.* GPS also conducted a three-month study of all the guest buggies used on the golf course in Banyan Tree Bintan and recommended the usage of solar panels. Subsequently, the roofs of all buggies were installed with solar panels. The photovoltaic panels extended the mileage between required charges, thus increasing the battery life by 35%. The successful implementation of solar panels in Bintan was replicated at Banyan Tree Ungasan.

- *Efficient Lighting.* Banyan Tree installed efficient lighting at many of its properties such as those in Lijiang, Vabbinfaru, Bangkok, Ihuru, Phuket and Maison Souvannaphoum. It also put in timers for public area air conditioning and carpark lighting in Bangkok, as well as garden lighting in Vabbinfaru, in order to reduce energy consumption.

- *Alternative water sources for landscape watering.* Water from draining tubs (greywater), captured rainwater and runoff, along with on-site wastewater treatment, is used to irrigate most of its properties.

- *Save Water.* Vabbinfaru placed sealed 1.5L bags in water cisterns to save 1.5L of water per flush. Phuket installed waterless urinals in all male public restrooms to save water that had been previously used for flushing.

- *Waste Separation.* Ungasan separates food wastes from other wastes, thus reducing the amount sent to landfills. This food waste is donated to a local duck breeder in Bintan and pig farmers in Mayakoba and Bangkok.

Banyan Tree aims to continue in its efforts to conserve natural resources. It has rolled out EarthCheck programs at all its resorts. EarthCheck is a leading benchmarking certification and environmental program that has been adopted by the travel and tourism industry (http://www.earthcheck.org/). The areas covered comprise energy consumption, greenhouse gas emissions, potable water consumption and water saving rating. Over the years, the Banyan Tree properties that have participated in the program have achieved positive results. For example, Banyan Tree Lijiang has attained the EarthCheck Silver Certification for four consecutive years since 2008.

☐ 'Empowering People'

Besides environmental projects and environmental resource conservation programs, Banyan Tree also finds ways to enhance the livelihood of those people living within the communities where it operates, through its 'Seedlings' initiative. 'Seedlings' was launched by Banyan Tree in 2007 and is a group-wide initiative to enhance the long-term prosperity of communities by cultivating their young people through programs including:

Mentoring programs

These programs identify young people between the ages of 12 and 18 within the local community who may be at risk of societal exclusion. Associates trained by the University of Wales are assigned as mentors to these young people. Structured topics that are used to guide mentor-mentee interactions include the discussion of relevant issues and topics in the key areas of society, environment, academic interests, health and sports.

Scholarships

Banyan Tree provides scholarships to young people who cannot afford an education. Upon the completion of their studies, the graduates are given the option of participating in Banyan Tree's internships. These internships are designed to provide the young people with job training and invaluable work experience. Interns have the opportunity to work in operational areas such as housekeeping, food and beverage, engineering, frontline customer service, marketing, reservations, procurement, security and landscape architecture.

Empowering People through Education

Recognising that education can enhance an individual's contribution to society, career options and sense of empowerment, Banyan Tree has engaged in a wide variety of efforts to support primary, secondary and tertiary education in host communities. Apart from its scholarships and internship programs, the company also organises field trips for students from Chi Heng Foundation to their property, Banyan Tree Hangzhou, to give young people a deeper understanding of the hospitality industry.

The company has also set up Practical Skills Training Centres for Women in China. These centres impart entrepreneurial skills to women who are involved in postpartum, neonatal and elderly care, so that these women could start their own businesses by better offering these services to the people within the community.

Empowering Communities

Fostering the long-term societal prosperity of communities is central to Banyan Tree's goal of creating value for community stakeholders; hence, it has offered its assistance whenever a need has arisen.

After the March 2011 Tohoku Quake and the ensuing tsunamis, Banyan Tree's associates, in combination with Banyan Tree's matching donations, raised over US$30,000 in support of the long-term recovery of affected communities. Banyan Tree donated the funds to Ashinaga, one of the largest non-profit education-focused organisations in Japan, in support of its Tohuku Rainbow House effort — the creation of a facility that provides psychological assistance to children who had lost one or both parents in the quake and the ensuing disaster.

In late 2011, Banyan Tree's associates, once again in combination with Banyan Tree's matching donations, generated a total sum of US$70,000 to help victims of the severe floods in Bangkok and other densely-populated areas in Thailand so that they could resume normalcy in their lives.

■ Future Outlook

Banyan Tree Hotels and Resorts will continue to pursue sustainable development as an agent of social and economic development through responsible tourism in the communities where their hotels, resorts and spas are located. Their future will exemplify commitment to their core values, corporate social responsibility and shared value. Banyan Tree's presence in 27 countries in environmentally sensitive locations around the world provides the tourism industry with an example of a company that embraces environmental conservation and fosters the empowerment of people in these communities.

■ Summary and Conclusion

Banyan Tree is a developer and manager of premium resorts, hotels, and spas committed to sustainable development. They have been conscientious in their endeavours to preserve the human and physical environment of all their properties around the world. Their conservation efforts are enshrined in their *core values*. *Corporate social responsibility* and *corporate shared value* are concepts demonstrated by Banyan Tree's sustainable development activities at Bang Tao Bay - Laguna Phuket and subsequent properties.

■ Study Questions

1 Outline and discuss the impacts of entrepreneurial strategic decision making and the core values of Executive Chairman, Mr Ho Kwon-Ping on the sustainable development of Bang Tao Bay - Laguna Phuket.

2 List and discuss how Banyan Tree builds and maintains value for its customers with their sustainable hotels and resorts.

3 List the sustainable best practices developed and implemented by Banyan Tree. Discuss why these best practices work well for Banyan Tree and why they may or may not work for other hotel companies.

4 Many of Banyan Tree's properties are luxury resorts. Analyse whether sustainability and luxury can coexist.

5 Describe whether Banyan Tree's corporate social responsibility programs demonstrate Porter & Kramer's concept of shared value.

Acknowledgement: The authors would like to acknowledge the contribution of **Michael Kwee** who is the Coordinating Director for Banyan Tree Global Foundation. Working with the Board of Directors based in Singapore, Michael is responsible for oversight, planning and management of all matters related to Banyan Tree Global Foundation.

■   References

Banyan Tree (2012) 'Banyan Tree Holdings Limited Annual Report 2011', retrieved from http://media.corporate-ir.net/Media_Files/IROL/20/200797/bth_annual_report_2011sgx.pdf on 27 March 2013.

Banyan Tree (2013a) 'History', retrieved from http://www.banyantreeglobalfoundation.com/about_us/history on 6 March 2013.

Banyan Tree (2013b) 'Sustainability Report 2006' retrieved from www.banyantree.com/downloads/pdf/.../banyan_tree_sr_2006.pdf on 6 March 2013.

Carroll, A. B. (1999) 'Corporate social responsibility evolution of a definitional construct' *Business & Society*, **38**(3), 268-295.

Harvard Kennedy School (2008) 'Corporate Social Responsibility Initiative: The initiative defining corporate social responsibility', retrieved from http://www.hks.harvard.edu/m-rcbg/CSRI/init_define.html on 6 March 2013.

Heathfield, S.M. (2013) 'Core values are what you believe', retrieved from http://humanresources.about.com/od/glossaryc/g/Core-Values.htm on 6 March 2013.

Laguna Phuket (2013) 'Ho Kwon Ping Biography', retrieved from http://www.lagunaphuket.com/media-hub/downloads/Ho-Kwon-Ping.pdf on 6 March 2013.

Levy, S.E. and Duverger, P. (2010) 'Consumer perceptions of sustainability in the lodging industry: Examination of sustainable tourism criteria', *International CHRIE conference-Refereed Track, Paper 31*, retrieved from http://scholarworks.umass.edu/refereed/CHRIE_2010/Friday/31 on 6 March 2013.

McMullen, J.S. and Shepherd, D.A. (2006) 'Entrepreneurial action and the role of uncertainty in the theory of the entrepreneur', *Academy of Management Review*, **31**, 132-152.

Patzelt, H. and Shepherd, D.A. (2010) 'Recognising opportunities for sustainable development', *Entrepreneurship Theory and Practice*, **35**(4), 631-652.

Porter, M.E. and Kramer, M.R. (2006) 'Strategy and society: The link between competitive advantage and corporate social responsibility', *Harvard Business Review*, **84** (12), 78-92.

Porter, M.E. and Kramer, M.R. (2011) 'Creating shared value', *Harvard Business Review*, **89**(1-2), 62-77.

United Nations (2010) 'Sustainable Development: From Brundtland to Rio 2012', retrieved from http://www.un.org/wcm/webdav/site/climatechange/shared/gsp/docs/GSP1-6_Background%20on%20Sustainable%20Devt.pdf on 6 March 2013.

7

8 Corporate Social Responsibility and the Sustainable Tourism Practices of Marriott International

Cynthia S. Deale, *East Carolina University*

Synopsis and Learning Outcomes

This case study focuses on the corporate social responsibility (CSR) practices of Marriott International, Inc., one of the world's largest lodging firms. The case discusses ways sustainable business concepts and procedures have been implemented into its strategies and operations, and emphasises its incorporation of CSR throughout its efforts. The company's successful participation in extensive CSR activities consists of applying the sustainable practices of safeguarding natural and cultural heritage, demonstrating social and economic benefits to local people, and engaging in environmentally friendly operations. Marriott's CSR efforts embrace three themes, using the triple bottom line (TBL) approach to sustainability, expressed in the company's core values as business, society, and environment (Marriott International, Inc., 2012). The company reports the social, economic, and environmental impacts of its sustainability efforts via the framework developed by the Global Reporting Initiative (GRI) (2013) and seeks to address the concerns of its varied stakeholders.

This case study briefly describes Marriott's sustainability practices, focusing on CSR. After completing this case study, learners should be able to:

1   Define basic concepts of CSR and how a company can apply these in its internal practices as well externally with a variety of partners

2 Describe the TBL approach to sustainability in lodging operations in terms of the interconnections between the economy, the natural environment, and the social and cultural realm, and specifically CSR.

3 Explain best practices for CSR that can be implemented in lodging operations.

4 Identify opportunities and challenges and the give and take involved in balancing the TBL approach to practicing sustainability in lodging operations, particularly while embracing CSR throughout an operation.

5 Suggest additional sustainability practices that would be useful and desirable in the future in lodging operations.

■ Background

□ The Company

Marriott International, Inc. began in 1927 in the United States (U.S.), when J. Willard Marriott and his wife opened a small root beer stand, later called the Hot Shoppe, in Washington, DC. In 1939, the Marriotts acquired their first food-service management contract with the U.S. Treasury, growing their business and Hot Shoppes, Inc. In 1957, they opened their first hotel in Virginia (Marriott International, Inc., 2012a). The corporate name of Hot Shoppes, Inc. was changed to the Marriott Corporation in 1967 and the business expanded into airline food service, food production, and lodging. In 1969, Marriott opened a hotel in Mexico, its first property outside of the U.S. In 1972, J.W. Marriott, Jr. was named Chief Executive Officer (CEO) and in 1975, the company opened its first European hotel, in Amsterdam. Marriott opened its 100th hotel in Hawaii in 1981, began the Courtyard concept in 1983, and entered the vacation time-share and senior-living segments of the industry in 1984 (Marriott, 1997). Marriott International, Inc. continues to expand and flourish, with over 3,700 lodging properties in 74 countries (Marriott News Center, 2013).

As of 2013, the company operates and franchises hotels under 18 brands; these include Marriott Hotels & Resorts, The Ritz-Carlton, JW Marriott, Bulgari, EDITION, Renaissance, Gaylord Hotels, Autograph Collection, AC Hotels by Marriott, Courtyard, Fairfield Inn & Suites, SpringHill Suites, Residence Inn, TownePlace Suites, Marriott Executive Apartments, Marriott Vacation Club, Grand Residences by Marriott, and The Ritz-Carlton Destination Club (Marriott News Center, 2013). To staff these properties, it employs more than 300,000 people around the world, at its headquarters or in managed and franchised properties. The company reported sales from continuing operations of $12 billion for the fiscal year 2011 (Marriott News Center, 2013).

☐ **Marriott's Sustainability Efforts**

The company's sustainability practices are widespread and substantial. In 2007, the company developed the Marriott Environmental Public Policy Statement and in its sustainability reports for the years of 2009 through 2012, Marriott cited accomplishments in the areas of immigration and integration, global diversity and inclusion, ethics and human rights, poverty alleviation, disaster relief efforts, vitality of children, the environment (energy, water, waste, carbon), green buildings, the supply chain, educating and inspiring associates and guests, and the 'Spirit to Preserve' - Juma Reserve and Nobility of Nature projects (Marriott International, Inc., 2009; 2010; 2012). In 2009 alone, the company celebrated its 10-year anniversary of the *Women's Leadership Development Initiative*, commemorated the 20-year anniversary of its formal programs to promote diversity and inclusion, expanded its portfolio of LEED-certified buildings to include more than 85 hotels and its global headquarters (Matthews, 2011), and was awarded the World Travel and Tourism Council (WTTC) 'Tourism for Tomorrow Award for Sustainability' (Marriott International, Inc., 2009).

It has continued to receive recognition for its sustainability efforts, including being chosen as one of the world's best companies for working women in 2012 (Working Mother, 2012), being ranked the top large hotel chain in terms of its sustainable business practices for three consecutive years (Climate Counts, 2012), and earning the 2013 Work-Life Seal of Distinction from the World at Work's Alliance for Work-Life Progress (AWLP) (Marriott News Center, 2013b). In addition, it has been repeatedly recognised as one of the best companies to work for by *FORTUNE* magazine and as one of the most environmentally friendly large companies in the U.S. by *Newsweek* magazine (Marriott News Center, 2013a).

■ Key Concepts

Several concepts underlie the sustainability efforts practiced by Marriott. These include fundamental components of **sustainable development** and CSR efforts, which are threaded throughout Marriott's sustainability initiatives and practices. In addition, Marriott's environmental vision and goals provide a context for the case. Background elements of sustainability that may be helpful for understanding this case, include:

- Definitions of sustainable development and sustainability (World Commission on Environment and Development,1987).

- Foundations of the TBL (triple bottom line) of sustainability (Elkington, 1997; Hawken, 2007: Hawken, 1993; Hawken *et al.*, 1999).

- A focus on employees and the community as keys to fostering and supporting the sustainability process (Senge, 2008).

- Reducing environmental impacts through the reduction of the **carbon footprint**.

- Using TBL sustainability reporting systems such as those developed by the **GRI** (Global Reporting Initiative) (2013),which include integrated reporting that combines the analysis of non-financial performance, comprised of CSR and environmental efforts, along with financial performance.

- Sustainability and the sustainable development process as a '**way of traveling**' rather than a destination (Harrison, 2000:p. 9; GRI, 2013).

- The significance of CSR to the well-being of a company and its **stakeholders**.

Viewing sustainability as a journey (GRI, 2013) or as '**a way of traveling**' (Harrison, 2000: p. 9), rather than as an endpoint, suggests that an organisation or company does not reach sustainability; instead sustainability is dynamic in nature. As Marriott has increased its brand portfolio and complexity, it shifts and adapts its sustainability focus to fit the needs of its various **stakeholders** in its efforts to address critical social, cultural, and economic issues. Stakeholders in Marriott consist of all those with interests in the firm who may receive benefits, although the interests and needs of these groups may not always be evident (Donaldson & Preston, 1995). These include associates, guests, franchisees, shareholders, communities, suppliers, industry organisations, government, and the wide range of organisations involved in sustainability efforts.

The European Commission (2001) defines **CSR** as "a concept whereby companies integrate social and environmental concerns in their business operations and in their interaction with their stakeholders on a voluntary basis," and Marriott engages in practices related to this concept throughout its operations around the globe. The John F. Kennedy School of Government's view of CSR is that "it goes beyond philanthropy and compliance and addresses how companies manage their economic, social, and environmental impacts, as well as their relationships in all key spheres of influence: the workplace, the marketplace, the supply chain, the community, and the public policy realm (Harvard University, 2013)." And as Porter and Kramer (2006) noted, "when a well-run business applies its vast resources, expertise, and management talent to problems that it understands and in which it has a stake, it can have a greater impact on social good than any other institution or philanthropic organisation (p. 92)." It is not surprising then to find out that Marriott has long been a champion of CSR within the company itself and via its philanthropic efforts in communities worldwide.

One of the company's focal environmental efforts areas has been to develop a program to help every guest reduce his or her **carbon footprint**, defined as "the amount of carbon emitted by something during a given period (Merriam-Webster Dictionary, 2012)." Starting in 2009, Marriott guests could make a contribution of a minimum of $10 (equivalent to 10 nights) to offset their carbon footprint online or via post. The company came up with the figure by calculating the electrical and gas consumption in guest rooms and public spaces in almost 1,000 of its properties as well as at its headquarters and regional office buildings. Marriott followed the World Resources Institute's Greenhouse Gas Protocol to generate its program and had it independently certified by ICF International, a climate change consulting service (JustGive, 2009; Marriott International, Inc., 2009).

To report the results of such sustainability projects, Marriott uses the reporting procedure of the **GRI** (2013), a systematic way to chronicle sustainability efforts, on an annual basis in a manner similar to the way that it reports its financial performance. The GRI has offered organisations around the world a framework for reporting sustainability since 1999. It consists of implementing a reporting cycle that involves data collection, communication, and responses. Due to its credibility, consistency, and comparability, the GRI framework has become widely accepted as a standard sustainability reporting system around the globe (GRI, 2013).

Marriott continues to pursue its current initiatives while striving to do even more as an effective global corporate citizen in environmental, societal, and business spheres. The company embraces a holistic view of CSR that comprises not just what the company does with its profits to benefit others, but also how it makes its money. It is evident that Marriott has a whole-hearted, whole company, every property - every employee - every guest kind of approach to sustainability. The following analysis demonstrates the company's dedicated efforts in all areas of sustainability.

■ Case Analysis

□ Marriott's Vision and Goals

The company strives to be the #1 hospitality company in the world and has a vision that focuses on a well-developed purpose; strongly held, clearly articulated, core values; up-to-date, comprehensive strategies; and well-defined measures of success (Marriott, International, Inc., 2012b). Marriott strives to "put people first" by taking care of its associates so that they can take care of customers and stresses pursuing excellence, embracing change, acting with integrity when it does business, and serving the world in a variety of constructive ways (Marriott International, Inc., 2012b). Its "spirit to serve" initiative focuses on how it works with communities to be active contributing members of the communities around the world where it operates, focusing on issues where Marriott can make a difference through using resources wisely, selecting good community partners, and enhancing its impacts on community needs (Marriott, 1997).

☐   ## CSR efforts

Marriott engages in numerous CSR endeavours (several of its significant CSR efforts are summarised in Table 8.1), collaborating with charitable organisations in communities around the world through addressing key SERVE issues of shelter and food (S), the environment (E), educating and training for hotel careers (R), promoting the vitality of children (V), and embracing global diversity and inclusion (E) (Center for Social Value Creation, 2010; Marriott, 1997). As an innovator in social and community programs, the firm started the *Marriott Foundation for People with Disabilities* to further the employment of young people with disabilities, and made its diversity strategy official in 1989. In 1990, it began *Pathways to Independence*, and its *Welfare to Work Program*, and since 1992, the company has collaborated with the organisation now called *Feeding America* to aid hunger relief (Marriott International, Inc., 2013).

Yet, Marriott engages in even more CSR initiatives. In 1995, Marriott formalised its partnership with *Habitat for Humanity* through its Fairfield Inn brand. The partnership, now extended to other brands, has resulted in donations of money and volunteer hours to construct of hundreds of homes for families in need. And in 1999, Marriott embarked on its *Women's Leadership Development Initiative* and hosted its first *National Women's Leadership Conference*, reinforcing the goal of increasing the number of women in leadership positions in the company (Marriott International, Inc., 2013).

In 2007, the company initiated the use of *Sed de Saber*, an English-education device to help Spanish-speaking employees learn to speak English (Marriott International, Inc., 2009). More recently, Marriott donated generously to disaster relief after the devastation of hurricane Sandy in the fall of 2012 in the north-eastern U.S. and devoted considerable time and effort to youth employment issues in the last year (CSRwire, 2012). One of its recent projects, A World of Opportunity, focuses specifically on the unemployment of youth in Europe, providing apprenticeships, training, and employment opportunities in its operations (Hospitality Net, 2012).

☐   ## Business Practices

Marriott's CSR theme is threaded through its business strategies, emphasising working partnerships with its associates around the globe to do business in ethical, sustainable ways. The company believes in a business model of managing and franchising hotels, such that at the end of 2011, 44 per cent of its hotels operated under management agreements and 53 per cent operated under franchise agreements (Marriott International, Inc., 2012). In its franchised properties, the company does not manage employees, building operations, or maintenance; instead, it collaborates with owners and franchisees to make certain that brand standards are met and that franchised properties benefit from the company's policies and programs.

Marriott's core business values include paying attention to its associates' well-being, guest satisfaction, human rights, global diversity and inclusion, economic hotel development, and stakeholders (Marriott International, Inc., 2012; 2013a). For example, the company embarked on a special health and wellness program for its associates called TakeCare in 2010. The TakeCare initiative engages associates as wellness champions at all locations to promote the program, introduces healthy activities such as eating better and exercising regularly, and fosters participation in wellness challenges (Marriott News Center, 2012). Marriott's founder, J. Willard Marriott counselled the company's managers to "take care of your employees and they'll take care of your customers" (Marriott, 1997; Marriott International, Inc., 2013b) and this philosophy is a driving force behind the company's ongoing sustainability journey.

Table 8.1: Selected Corporate Social Responsibility efforts of Marriott International. Inc.

Business Values

Principles:

- World-class service
- Ethical business practices
- Commitment to employees
- Commitment to the company's culture
- Policies on employment
- Policies on human rights
- Policy on the environment
- Policy on the supply chain
- Conduct the company upholds and expects of others

Examples:

- It stands against human trafficking and the exploitation of children, does not recruit child labour, and works to raise awareness concerning such crimes
- It conducts training on human rights, including the protection of children, for all associates worldwide
- It advises managers and associates on laws relating to antitrust, unfair competition, political contributions, abuse of purchasing power, commercial and political bribery, etc.
- It conducts business ethics training programs worldwide

Environment

Goals:

- Further reduce energy and water consumption 20% by 2020
- Empower hotel development partners to build green hotels
- Green multi-billion dollar supply chain
- Educate and inspire associates and guests to conserve and preserve
- Address environmental challenges through innovative conservation initiatives including rainforest protection and water conservation

Examples:

- Developing LEED certified properties across all brands.
- Electrical consumption at its headquarters has been reduced 9.04% since 2007
- First major hotel chain to calculate its carbon footprint (59.4 pounds of CO_2e per available room)
- Increased its landfill diversion rates in the US by 6% since 2010
- Adopted a climate-specific landscape approach, including rain sensor installations in 194 hotels
- Developed retro-commissioning program
- Juma rainforest conservation project

Society

Norms:

- Associates have access to support and workplace training to enhance emotional and physical well-being
- It extends its role to provide shelter and food, especially during times of disaster
- It promotes and nurtures community social well-being through partnerships, donations, and volunteerism with international, national, and local charitable organisations

Examples:

- In 2010, its worldwide charitable contributions totalled $34.6 million from donations of cash, in-kind and volunteer time
- Affiliations include Habitat for Humanity International, Feeding America, the International Federation of Red Cross & Red Crescent Societies and the American Red Cross
- Its properties are encouraged to develop partnerships in their own communities
- It offers educational opportunities for young people interested in careers in hospitality and addressing youth employment issues Source: Marriott International, Inc. (2013c; 2012c).

☐   # Environmental stewardship

Marriott's environmental efforts are integral to the company's business values, such that green hotel practices comprise a significant component of its CSR philosophies and practices (Marriott International, Inc., 2013a) (see Table 8.1). In 2006, Marriott introduced its first annual 'Environmental Awareness Month' to encourage actions to conserve the natural environment and decrease the use of resources, and all properties in the U.S. and Canada became smoke-free. Environmental practices related directly to how Marriott does business include increasing its collection of green hotels and receiving the Sustained Excellence Award several times from the U.S. Environmental Protection Agency (EPA). The EPA has awarded its ENERGY STAR (R) label to approximately 275 Marriott hotels, more than any other hotel company at the time. Another accomplishment involves greening its $10 billion supply chain by replacing plastic key cards, towels, pens, toilet paper, pillows, and paint with more environmentally-friendly items (PR Newswire, 2009; Marriott, International, Inc., 2009).

As noted, one of the company's accomplishments includes allowing guests to reduce their carbon footprints to help offset the carbon generated during their stay. The donations accepted to reduce guests' carbon footprints help to fund Marriott's Juma project focused on rainforest education and conservation as part of the *Amazonas Sustainable Foundation* in Brazil (ASFB) (JustGive, 2009). The *Amazonas Initiative and the Juma Reduction of Emissions from Deforestation and Forest Degradation (REDD+) Project* piloted an approach to conservation and wise use of resources to catalyse sustainable social and economic development, which protects the forest, assesses avoided deforestation, and commercialises verified emission reductions (Zadek *et al.*, 2012). The project began with funds generated through a state endowment, philanthropic contributions, and via the carbon-offset program marketed to Marriott hotel guests. The project has acquired significant donations through Marriott's *Spirit to Preserve* group meetings promotional program (PR Newswire, 2009; Marriott, International, Inc., 2009; Zadek *et al.*, 2012), and involves educating and working with about 450 local families of the rainforest to educate them that the forest is worth more standing than cut, and who receive payments in recognition of their roles as stewards of the forest. Initial results of the project are positive; however, it is still in its pilot phase with challenges such as the realisation that the project may not necessarily support the co-benefits of poverty alleviation and the creation of sustainable livelihoods, or the spread of benefits to other forest areas (Zadek *et al.*, 2012).

Marriott also supports legislation focusing on climate and energy challenges, believing that agreement on climate legislation and global energy security is needed to ensure a sustainable future. The company continues to tackle issues raised by climate change through its business strategies and internal policies

8

and practices. While climate change legislation is currently on hold in the U.S., Marriott continues to work on its efforts to advocate for legislation that rewards ongoing energy-related initiatives and tropical rainforest conservation projects. It also approves of and actively supports the World Travel and Tourism Council's (WTTC) Action Agenda to encourage efforts to address climate change and participates as an industry partner with the WTTC (World Travel and Tourism Council, n.d.; Marriott International, Inc., 2012).

☐ Future Outlook

The future outlook for Marriott in the area of sustainability is bright. For example, the company continues to be recognised for its leadership in social responsibility by being named again as a member company of the Financial Times Stock Exchange (FTSE) FTSE4Good Index Series for 2011, a designation it has held since the beginning of the index in 2002 (FSTE Group, n.d., Marriott International, Inc., 2012). Marriot also received the U.S. Postal Service's 2011 Supplier Sustainability Excellence Award for its outstanding supply chain performance (Marriott International, Inc., 2012). In addition, under the leadership of J.W. Marriott, Jr., the Executive Chairman, and Arne Sorenson, the President and Chief Executive Officer of the company, Marriott has expanded its sustainability efforts (Marriott International, Inc., 2012). Efforts include, but are not limited to, starting a global careers site to attract world-class talent, addressing the worldwide youth employment situation, launching an executive-level Global Diversity and Inclusion Council, actively investing in a water conservation program in Southwest China, and participating in a sustainable seafood program called *FutureFish* for its hotels around the world (Marriott International, Inc., 2012).

■ Summary and Conclusion

Marriott continues its efforts in its hotels to reduce energy and water consumption, waste production, and the carbon footprint; improve the supply chain; expand its number of green hotels; and engage guests and associates in sustainable practices. Marriott has also received recognition as an environmental leader in the hotel industry from several industry-related groups, including Ceres, an association of investors and environmentalists, the non-profit organisation ClimateCounts.org, and Travel and Leisure magazine (Hotel News Resource, 2009; PR Newswire, 2009;Marriott International, 2012). At the same time, it is extending its efforts beyond its hotels to embrace rainforest preservation and water conservation (Marriott International, Inc., 2012d). An important endeavour in this area is Marriott's Juma REDD+ Project, mentioned previously as an innovative initiative to educate and value the forest-related contributions of local residents in reducing emissions and enhancing carbon stocks (Zadek *et al.*, 2012). Marriott continues to update and upgrade its sustainability efforts, not resting on its past accomplishments, but instead pushing forward to improve and expand upon its work in all areas of sustainability.

The quest for sustainability endures and Marriott continues to act in positive ways to enhance its sustainability efforts through a variety of CSR initiatives. As Harrison (2000:9) noted, and as the people of the Marriott company would probably agree, sustainability and the sustainable development process comprise a 'way of travelling' rather than a destination. Marriott focuses not only on pursuing what has been called company-centric sustainability; it emphasises sustainability of the larger system of which it is a part and upon which it depends, recognising interdependencies and working to reduce the fragmentation among all those who are concerned with TBL sustainability (Mohrman & Worley, 2012), and realising that CSR, like sustainability, is an ongoing journey.

■ Study Questions

1   Sometimes there is resistance to practicing social and environmental sustainability in CSR efforts because these practices must be balanced with profitability. What can various stakeholders do to help ensure that this balance — the TBL of people-planet-profits -- is the focus of sustainability efforts?

2   Compare and contrast Marriott's CSR efforts with those of another prominent lodging or hospitality company. Use references to make the comparison.

3   One focus of sustainability is to buy local and fair trade goods, including foods, beverages, household goods, and furniture. Write a plan for purchasing for the lodging industry, or another segment of the hospitality and tourism industry, based on current and future trends in the global economy, with a focus on CSR and the TBL of sustainability. Cite at least two references.

4   Globalisation often refers to the increased mobility of goods, services, labour, technology, and capital throughout the world and this process has increased dramatically with the advent of new technologies. This interconnectedness increases interdependence and can create greater uniformity across cultures and societies and promote greater unity and openness (Gizewski, 2009). Discuss the benefits and drawbacks to this globalisation for CSR among those who operate hospitality and tourism businesses. Cite at least two references.

5   Marriott's CSR efforts are well integrated into its company culture and extensive. Suggest CSR efforts that you might engage in if you were the manager of a lodging operation. Base your ideas on what you had read about Marriott's CSR efforts, extend your ideas using material from at least two other companies, and explain why you believe that these CSR efforts would be effective.

8

■ Suggested Reading and Websites of Interest

Center for Sustainable Tourism (2012) Available at: www.sustainabletourism.org.

Green Meeting Industry Council (2012) Available at: www.greenmeetings.info/.

Green Seal (2012) Available at: www.greenseal.org.

Levy, S.E., Stuart, E. & Park, S. (2011) 'An analysis of CSR activities in the lodging industry', *Journal of Hospitality & Tourism Management*, **18** (1), 147-154.

Marriott International, Inc. (2013) 'About Marriott international: A world of opportunity', available at: http://www.marriott.com/marriott/aboutmarriott.mi.

Marriott International, Inc. (2012) 'Marriott sustainability report 2011-2012', available at: http://www.marriott.com/corporate-social-responsibility/corporate-responsibility.mi.

Porter, M.E. & Kramer, M.R. (2006) 'The link between competitive advantage and corporate social responsibility', *Harvard business review*, **84** (12), 78-92.

Sustainable Communities Network (SCN) (2012) available at:www.sustainable.org.

Sustainable Table (2013) available at: www.sustainabletable.org.

Sustainable Travel International (STI) (2013) available at: www.sustainabletravelinternational.org.

United Nations Educational, Scientific, and Cultural Organisation (UNESCO) (2012) available at: www.unesco.org.

INTERNATIONAL CASES IN SUSTAINABLE TRAVEL & TOURISM

PART 3

Zakynthos: Supply Chain Management and Customers' Involvement in Tourism Sustainability

Marianna Sigala, *University of the Aegean*

Synopsis and Learning Outcomes

This case study examines the collaborative sustainable practices adopted by three vertically integrated and sister organisations namely: Ionian Eco Villagers, Nature World Travel and Earth, Sea & Sky. The organisations are located in Zakynthos and aim to promote tourism development, while simultaneously protecting the marine life of the island. The analysis and examples of the case study explain how organisations can design, control, promote and provide a holistic sustainable tourism experience that creates shared value for all stakeholders involved by exploiting two issues: a) the vertical integration of the organisations through the tourism supply chain; and b) the creation of a stakeholders' network (including tourists, partners, suppliers, locals, volunteers, NGOs etc.) for developing collaborative sustainable practices. In analysing these approaches, the case study builds on theories related to: sustainable management based on a supply chain approach; shared (social, economic and environmental) value creation; and managing customer/people's behaviour and contributions towards sustainability. Finally, the case study discusses the affordances of social media to further enrich and expand the sustainable practices of the organisations at a global and wholly collaborative scale.

After completing this case study learners should be able to demonstrate:

1 The importance of managing sustainability from a tourism supply chain perspective.

2   The need to develop and nurture a stakeholder network for developing and implementing collaborative sustainable practices that create shared economic, social and environmental value to all stakeholders.

3   The importance of tourist roles and behaviour in achieving and supporting tourism sustainability.

4   The affordances of social media to enrich, expand and nurture the sustainable collaborative practices of organisations as well as to further empower customers to get actively involved in sustainability.

■ Background

Yannis Vardakastanis is the founder, owner and manager of three sister organisations; namely Ionian Eco Villages, Nature World Travel and Earth, Sea and Sky (http://www.relaxing-holidays.com/), which are based in Gerakas peninsula on the island of Zakynthos, Greece (Figures 8.1 and 8.2). These three vertically integrated organisations work together in order to create and provide unique, authentic and green holiday experiences in Zankynthos by supporting conservation, eco-friendly activities, education and immersion in local culture. In this vein, the promotion, protection and preservation of the rich natural flora and fauna of Zakynthos and the Ionian Islands are at the heart of the mission statement and strategy of the organisations.

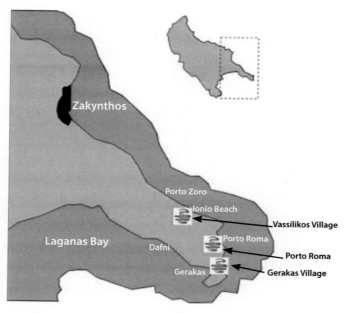

Figure 9.1: Location of the eco-lodges operated by the Ionian Eco Villagers at Gerakas Peninsula
Source: http://www.relaxing-holidays.com

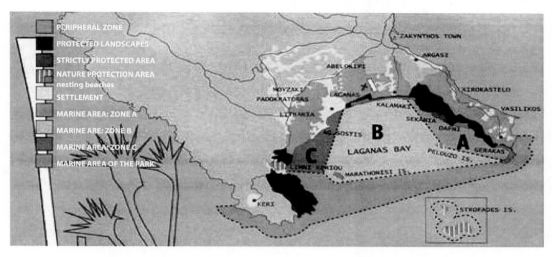

Figure 9.2: The National Marine Park of Zakynthos: Laganas Bay and Gerakas Peninsula
Source: http://www.natureworldtravel.com/marine_park.htm

Zakynthos is a vital but fragile ecosystem, as 80% of the population of the endangered species *Caretta Caretta* (the Loggerhead Sea Turtle) living in the Mediterranean nests on the beaches of Laganas Bay. Because of that, and after long-term intense lobbying from several concerned conservation groups, such as Medasset, Archelon STPS, and the WWF, a Presidential Decree was passed by the Greek Government in 1999 to establish the National Marine Park of Zakynthos (NMPZ) (http://www.nmp-zak.org/) in order to protect the sea turtles. The NMPZ includes (Figure 9.2): three marine zones A, B and C in the Bay of Laganas; strictly protected nesting areas; and protected terrestrial zones and peripheral areas. Several activities, such as fishing and building, are restricted in the NMPZ for the protection of the ecosystem (Table 9.1).

9

Table 9.1: Restriction of activities in the National Marine Park of Zakynthos (NMPZ)

Area	Restriction
Zone A	No-go area for boats; no fishing
Zone B	Boat speed up to 6 knots; no anchoring; no fishing
Zone C	Boat speed up to 6 knots; anchoring permitted; no fishing
Nesting beaches	Limits on the number of sub beds and umbrellas
	Sun beds and umbrellas must be stacked each night to give turtles access to the soft sand at the back of the beaches
	No access to the public between 7pm and 7am to stop the turtles being disturbed
	Wardens patrol the beaches 24h a day to inform tourists and also to stop people using the beaches after dark
	Existence of information boards and vehicle access barriers on each nesting beach
	No building on or behind nesting beaches of the NMPZ; this limits light pollution from buildings seeping on to the beaches which disturbs nesting turtles and disorientates hatchlings

Yannis Vardakastanis became a full time conservationist in 1991 when he moved his bar off the Gerakas nesting beach. Since then, he has been developing a series of sustainable organisations in order to promote sustainable tourism development which balances the needs of holiday makers and local tourism enterprises with those of the marine life of Zakynthos. In 1993, he funded the Ionian Eco Villagers (IEV), the first ever tour operator in Zakynthos offering eco-lodging on Zakynthos. Soon after, the business was expanded with the establishment of Nature World Travel (NWT) (http://www.natureworldtravel.com/) and a non-governmental organisation (NGO), namely Earth, Sea and Sky (ESS) (http://www.earthseasky.org/). NWT focuses on providing sustainable island excursions on Zakynthos, while ESS aims at supporting and fostering conservation work by building a global volunteer network. In 1996, ESS funded and built the Sea Turtle & Wildlife Information Centre at Gerakas – the only one on the island – to educate and encourage visitors to learn and protect the rich heritage, natural beauty, wildlife and culture of Zakynthos, and to promote the need for sustainable tourism. The organisations have three permanent staff members, employ several locals during the high season, and are assisted by numerous international volunteers working on the conservation programs.

Overall, the organisations represent a small tourism operator specialising in providing customised sustainable holidays in the NMPZ that may include:

- Accommodation in locally owned establishments that are part of the IEV network.
- Authentic local experiences combining volunteer conservation programs through the ESS.
- Eco-friendly activities and excursions developed by the NWT.
- Sea turtle and marine life educational opportunities.

The goal of the organisations is to fight against the development and damage of mass tourism in Greece, and specifically on Zakynthos, by minimising the negative impacts of tourism on the environment, undertaking conservation work on the ground, and informing visitors and local businesses of the unique flora and fauna found in Zakynthos and the importance of safeguarding them. The commitment of the organisations to achieving long-term sustainable eco-tourism is clearly evident in the way they have drafted and follow their responsible tourism policy (Relaxing Holidays, 2012, that states: ' … by writing a responsible tourism policy, we wish to continually improve the way in which we run our business to the benefit of everyone involved: our business and our customers, local people and beautiful Gerakas'. Indeed, the key success factor and distinctive advantage of the organisations relies on their abilities:

1   To design and control the provision of a holistic sustainable tourism experience

covering almost all tourism services (i.e. accommodation, activities, excursions, education).

2   To influence and direct the behaviour of numerous stakeholders (e.g. tourists, locals, volunteers, professionals, governments) towards a sustainable code of conduct that creates win-win situations which benefit everyone.

The ability of the three sister organisations to produce multi-dimensional and multi-stakeholder sustainable impacts is heavily dependent on their vertical integration and diversification of activities in various aspects of tourism experiences and daily life.

Several facts, numbers and awards demonstrate the significant results of the sustainable efforts of the organisation. Tireless lobbying efforts have forced the Greek Government to enact a responsible development policy and require responsible operating procedures from the existing tourism businesses in the proximity of turtle nesting beaches. Hence, the area of the NMPZ is still untouched by development:

■   Bars, restaurants and other businesses are not developed in nesting beaches.

■   There are no pedaloes or canoes for hire on the beach; visitors' numbers are controlled with time limits.

■   The number of sunbeds in Gerakas beach has been reduced from approximately 180 to 100.

■   More than 60% of visitors have become aware of the basic steps to avoid impacting on *Caretta Caretta* nesting, i.e. removing all litter including cigarette ends, staying within 5 meters of water.

As a result, the previously decreasing number of Loggerhead turtle nests on Gerekas Beach has stabilised for two years running during 2007 and 2008. In 2009, the organisation was selected as a finalist for the Conservation Award in the prestigious Tourism for Tomorrow Awards, while it has also received a Highly Commended award from First Choice in 2005 and a Highly Commended in Responsible Tourism award by Virgin Holidays in 2007. Numerous mass media agencies have also recognised and promoted the sustainable efforts of the organisation, including: *The Times*, *The Guardian* and documentaries by TV channels such as the BBC, Channel 4 and Documentary TV Japan.

■   Key Concepts

The three sister organisations represent a **sustainable enterprise**, as they follow business strategies, activities, processes and services that meet the needs of the enterprise and its **stakeholders** in the short term while protecting and enhancing human and natural resources for future generations.

Yannis Vardakastanis, the founder and owner of the organisations, can be characterised as a **social entrepreneur**, as he manages and operates his organisations with a social mission that features the following characteristics (Sloan *et al.*, 2013):

- Priority in the creation of social and shared value. Shared value is defined as policies and operating practices that enhance the competitiveness of an organisation while simultaneously advancing economic and social conditions in the communities in which it operates (Porter & Kramer, 2011). Indeed, the ultimate goal of Mr Vardakastanis is not to solely produce returns for him, but to also optimise returns to all stakeholders.

- Foster and support the implementation of social change for achieving a more sustainable world.

- Assessment of organisational success in terms of its impact on the society and not only based on financial returns.

Social entrepreneurs find numerous opportunities to act and prosper where a social need exists and when governments cannot or do not provide any solutions. Unfortunately, the highly bureaucratic and inflexible structures of Greek governmental organisations have resulted in the failure to quickly respond and provide sufficient protection to the fragile ecosystem of Zakynthos. The urgency of the problem, coupled with rapid and unplanned tourism development in the area, presented the opportunity to a young, energetic and sensitive entrepreneur, Yanni Vardakastani, to actively engage and lead sustainable practices on Zakynthos. However, Yannis Vardakastanis finds it more and more difficult to find and persuade public and private organisations to sponsor and financially support his sustainable practices because of many reasons including the economic crisis, tight corporate budgets and the need of firms to more effectively justify the returns of their social responsibility programmes.

In order to create social value, organisations have to find and adopt new governance and business models. Porter and Kramer (2011) claim that organisations can create shared social value by identifying and expanding the connections and partnerships between societal and economic progress. Generally, shared value can be created by using three innovative tools (Cronin *et al.*, 2011; Porter & Kramer, 2011; Sigala, 2008):

- The creation of market 'ecosystems' that will enable organisations to collaborate and form partnerships with many stakeholders (such as NGOs, governments, activists groups, citizens, suppliers etc.) in order to have a greater, holistic and sustainable social impact.

- The expansion of **value chains** in order to enable organisations to support sustainability not only by managing internal operations, but also by influencing the business processes that go beyond their organisational borders and are affected by third party organisations such as suppliers, partners and governments. To that end, many businesses currently implement and manage sustainability from a *supply chain management* (SCM) approach that considers the activities of all organisations in their business network.

■ The creation of new industrial clusters or networks whereby collaborative multi-stakeholder and easily controllable sustainable practices can be developed.

In tourism, sustainable management from a SCM and multi-stakeholder approach is a high priority, because tourism is an amalgam of many products provided by various firms (e.g. accommodation and catering providers, transportation, excursions). Hence, the creation of collaborative sustainable practices amongst all stakeholders involved in the tourism experience is widely advocated as the most appropriate way to address and achieve sustainability in the whole tourism ecosystem (Schwartz *et al.*, 2008; Kernel, 2005; Fadeeva, 2004 & 2005; Morrison *et al.*, 2004; TOI, 2007; Budeanu, 2005; Tepelus, 2005).

Studies have also recognised the important and active role that tourists play in ensuring sustainability (Sigala, 2010). Tourists participate in tourism during the purchase and consumption stage. By preferring and buying sustainable tourism products (even at higher prices), tourists contribute to and support the sustainable practices of tourism organisations. Moreover, the tourists' behaviour at the stage of consumption can also support or inhibit sustainable practices (e.g. tourists recycling garbage at destinations or not requesting their hotel towels to be changed on a daily basis). Increasingly, social media further empowers travellers and their social networks to actively participate in sustainability by collecting, sharing and disseminating knowledge about sustainability as well as by organising and participating in collective sustainable practices. Hence, the customers' values, lifestyles, education and awareness in demanding sustainable services, ideologies, purchasing decisions and behaviours can have a significant impact on the adoption of sustainable practices (McKercher & Prideaux, 2011; Mair, 2011). Overall, tourists are recognised as an important stakeholder group which can critically contribute to sustainability as co-designers, co-producers and co-marketers of sustainable practices and tourism services (Sigala, 2010).

Indeed, a new market segment usually referred to with the acronym LOHAS (Lifestyles of Health and Sustainability) has made its appearance (Sloan *et al.*, 2013). These customers are usually referred to as culturally creative and conscious consumers and they represent a sizeable group of customers in numerous western and developed countries. Numerous frameworks have been developed in order to explain the decision making process of LOHAS, but in general four factors are widely agreed to influence the motivation of **responsible consumerism** (Choi

9

et al., 2009): personal health and well-being; ecology (e.g. price, promotion and production methods of products/services); ethics; and lifestyle (e.g. practicality, prestige, social image and personality, self-esteem etc.).

A new consumer called the 'engaged consumer' has also emerged (Sigala, 2010) and is characterised by a willingness to get more actively involved in sustainability by recognising its role and impact beyond the consumption stage. Two types of engaged consumers can be identified (Sloan *et al.*, 2013):

■ The *activists*, who engage in sustainable behaviours, for example through recycling, changing consumption habits, becoming volunteers, participating in social/eco projects, leading and organising collective movements.

■ The *informed consumers*, who are more inclined towards searching for and disseminating information about sustainability rather than taking part in actions. Informed consumers will spend time in searching for information about the production processes of services/products and raising social awareness within a community, but they will not act at a political level.

By using several examples of actions, the following section further analyses how the three sister organisations owned by Yannis Vardakastanis implement sustainability by developing collaborative practices that require the active participation of several stakeholders involved in the tourism supply chain, such as the tourists, local residents and professionals, associations and (non)-governmental bodies.

■ Case Analysis

Implementing sustainability from a SCM approach requires firms to adopt sustainability principles and practices in all SC processes including product design, procurement, production, distribution and reverse logistics (Sigala, 2008). Table 9.2 provides the aims of each SCM process in order to become sustainable as well as some examples of sustainability practices adopted by Mr Vardakastanis' organisations. The fact that the three sister companies are vertically integrated and operate at different stages of the tourism supply chain (i.e. IEV operates at the accommodation production stage, NWT at the distribution stage and ESS at the destination management stage) enables Mr Vardakastanis to control, influence and co-ordinate sustainable practices along the whole supply chain in order to ensure that tourists can experience and actively participate in the co-production of a holistic sustainable tourism experience.

More examples showing how the three sister organisations collaborate with other stakeholders in their value chain for implementing sustainable practices that create shared (economic, social and/or environmental) value for everyone are analysed in depth below.

Table 9.2: Achieving sustainability from a supply chain management approach

Sustainability goals	Examples of sustainable practices
Sustainable Product Design	
Design and creation of a sustainable tourism product, e.g.: • Inclusion and selection only of sustainable suppliers • Design of tourist activities at destinations that aim to educate tourists and influence their behaviour towards the protection of environmental resources	Supporting local accommodation providers to design and provide environmental friendly products, e.g. solar heating, energy saving bulbs, no swimming pools Use of eco-friendly catamaran cruises Nature walks for educating and informing tourists about the local fauna and flora
Sustainable Procurement	
Development of tour packages that include sustainable tourism services/products: to achieve that the firm needs to carefully select the various suppliers and stakeholders (e.g. tour guides, public authorities) with which it will cooperate to develop the tour package	Use of local accommodation providers Protection and conservation of local culture and nature Free hire of bicycles to explore the island
Sustainable Production	
Tourism consumption takes places at the destination whereby many stakeholders are involved, Sustainable management of: • tourism destinations • the organisations' internal processes (e.g. tour operator business, accommodation, transportation, tour guides etc.) • tourists (e.g. awareness – education)	Use of volunteers in excursions for informing and controlling tourists' behaviour Volunteers cleaning up beaches Minimum printing (e.g. brochures, electronic communication and transactions) and minimum use of energy Free hire of beach umbrellas, towels and inflatable beds (eliminating purchase and throwing away of these items)
Sustainable Delivery – Distribution	
The use and management of a tourism distribution system and intermediaries that support sustainability, e.g. retail networks, travel agents and tour operators	Mr Vardakastanis created Green Tree Transfers, which specialises in sustainable distribution and logistics services by offering private airport transfers and car hire. For every leg of a transfer or taxi trip booked through this, the organisation plants a tree on Zakynthos. NWT is a sustainable focused tour operator, that focuses on the design, distribution and promotion of sustainable holiday packages and experiences in Zakynthos. When traveling to Zakynthos, NWT offers travellers off-setting purchase options for trading off their carbon emissions
Sustainable Reverse Logistics	
Measuring sustainability performance and usage of feedback mechanisms for monitoring and tracking performance and enabling learning and continuous improvement Tourists and volunteers are encouraged to adopt a sustainable lifestyle after their visit on Zakynthos	The organisation monitors and measure annual sustainability performance. Annual Assessment Reports are produced and disseminated to inform and motivate further action as well as create wider awareness towards sustainability The organisations exploit social media for: engaging and motivating tourists and volunteers to share their experiences on Zakynthos with others; promoting and disseminating sustainability concerns; and creating and participating in virtual communities that aim to support collaborative sustainable practices.

Source: adapted from Sigala (2008)

9

☐   Ionian Eco Villagers (IEV)

IEV are the operators responsible for providing environmentally friendly accommodation on Zakynthos. The operator manages and uses only small locally-owned accommodation properties (never large hotels) in order to manage the number of people to Gerakas at any one time: 15 small cottages and studio apartments, owned by local families, provide the accommodation for up to 60 people at any one time. IEV has clearly created a loyal customer base, as 80% of the guests return to this tranquil and untouched area for their annual holidays. The local economy has also benefited by employing only local people, supporting and recommending local firms (e.g. restaurants, car hire, artists) and procuring food supplies (e.g. turkey, goat, pigs, sheep and chickens) from locals that raise them using free-range and organic methods. Guests are directed to use only local guide services and local eco-friendly excursion companies. IEV consults with holiday property owners in order to help them to follow environmentally friendly practices such as using solar heating, energy-saving bulbs, energy and water saving practices (tanks capturing the rainwater), eco-friendly cleaning products, and not using pesticides or insecticides in gardens or providing swimming pools. By supporting the competitive management and promotion of local accommodation providers, the firm also helps in dissuading large hotel operators from buying land and developing large properties in the area. IEV also assists accommodation providers to regularly monitor and measure their standards and further improve them. The profits of the IEV are invested straight back into the conservation network of Mr Vardakastanis' organisations.

Guest education and active engagement in local conservation work are issues of a high importance for the IEV. Guests become aware before they arrive that they will be staying in a conservation area with endangered sea turtles, monk seals and other flora and fauna. Upon arrival guests are invited to attend a one hour one-on-one family education session with an ESS volunteer to provide necessary information on the local area, activities and, most importantly, protocols and tips for staying within the NMPZ. Guests are advised to save water and electricity and to minimise the use of air conditioning while at their accommodation. Guests are also encouraged to become actively involved in the conservation of Gerakas by offering them discounts when they participate in voluntary work during their stay. They are also urged to visit the Information centre of ESS at Gerakas, talk to volunteers and complain to the Tourist Police if they witness any illegal hunting.

The IEV also exerts a great deal of pressure on the Greek Government to develop and enforce environmental policies in the NMPZ. For example, although building is not permitted by law on or behind the turtle nesting beaches, some buildings have continued to be constructed. As a result, IEV along with other conservation groups helped to secure the imposition of a fine by the EU against the Greek

Government for failing to enforce the existing legislation. In 2006, IEV lobbied the Government to prevent tourists from hacking away at the unique, mineral-rich clay cliffs found on Zakynthos. This practice was causing irreparable damage to the island's natural habitat, speeding up erosion and degrading the cliffs. The area is now signposted and roped-off, providing protection to the unique cliff formations. IEV also helped to secure nocturnal light and noise restrictions at beachside bars and hotels in Laganas' nesting beaches.

☐ Nature World Travel (NWT)

NWT is a tour operator focusing on the design, distribution and promotion of sustainable holiday packages in Zakynthos. Hence, its role in supporting sustainability in the tourism supply chain is critical as it can direct and support local tourism suppliers to become more sustainable; and it can influence and motivate appropriate tourist behaviour before and during their holidays in Zakynthos towards using sustainable suppliers and protecting the local ecosystem (Sigala, 2008). The ecosystem of Zakynthos represents a major part of the 'product' that NWT sells to its customers. Consequently, its protection is regarded as a vital duty. One of the best ways to protect the ecosystem is to create activities that justify its existence and protection, as well as generating income to conserve it. For example, in order to oppose hunting, the NWT promotes bird watching and rambling activities throughout the Ionian Sea region in order to extend the tourist season, increase tourist spending on the island, create jobs for locals and provide an alternative to uncontrolled hunting.

To that end, NWT designs and promotes only sustainable excursions and tourist activities, such as: eco-tourism catamaran cruises and jeep safari tours by a sustainable local company; nature walks and guided snorkelling trips; and traditional Greek evenings. During the summer months, NWT employs native Ionians to operate non-intrusive wildlife excursions such as regular turtle-watching boat trips and nature rambles around the Gerakas headland to observe a pod of monk seals and see some of the rare wild flowers. NWT also facilitates cultural events and visits to a traditional winery and ancient Zakynthian mountain villages. The major purpose of these activities is to meet some of the local people, learn and preserve the local culture, admire some of the architectural icons of the island and more crucially, to generate a small amount of extra income for the agricultural population located at the more rural (non-tourist developed) areas of Zakynthos.

During the excursions, qualified ESS volunteers escort small groups of tourists who have the opportunity to learn about and get first-hand experience of the fragile local ecosystem. Tourists are obliged to adhere to an eco-protocol that is aligned with the laws of the NMPZ (e.g. no swimming with the turtles, no making noise to attract turtles' attention). (Read more of the tourists' code of conduct at http://www.natureworldtravel.com/turtle_friendly.htm).

NWT believes that bringing environmental awareness to the tourists is half of the battle in the bid to protect the turtles. But apart from simply educating tourists, NWT organises activities in which tourists are empowered to become the co-producers and the co-marketers of tasks that help promote and raise funds for sustainability. For example, nature and photography walks are organised whereby tourists learn about the ecosystem but also how to take excellent pictures. A Nature Photo competition is organised in order to motivate participation. The winner receives a gift certificate (a pack of eco-friendly products), while the winning image is printed as a postcard that is distributed by ESS as part of its fundraising campaign. Indeed, research has shown that to motivate and influence customers' sustainable behaviour, organisations can use instrumental mechanisms (i.e. the provision of financial benefits such as reductions and awards to customers adopting sustainable practices) and/or normative controls (e.g. peer recognition of customers' good behaviour) (Goldstein *et al.* 2008; Terry *et al.*, 1999). A significant part of NWT's income is also donated to the NMPZ.

☐ Earth, Sea & Sky (ESS)

ESS is a non-governmental-organisation (NGO) whose major role is to protect the marine ecosystem of the NMPZ. For example, ESS organises conservation work such as beach clean-ups in which tourists, locals and other volunteers are encouraged to participate. At Gerekas Bay, ESS have had trade stalls removed from the beach, the beds and umbrellas are restricted to a small area and removed at night, the beach is closed to the public at night and a car park was removed from the area directly above the beach. ESS funds each of its activities through donations from IEV, NWT, visitors and various international fund raising efforts.

ESS has established two non-profit facilities in Gerakas: a Wildlife Information Centre and Aquarium and an SOS Sea Turtle Rescue Centre (http://earth-sea-sky-global.org/turtle-rescue-centre). The Information Centre employs staff and volunteers who inform visitors about turtles and other wildlife, teach how to protect nests and hatchlings, remind people they are visiting a protected area and ask them to respect the laws of the NMPZ. Specialised workshops and seminars aimed at building environmental education are also organised; for example, the centre runs workshops for children and adults about making bird, insect and mammal houses and feeders by utilising recycled and reclaimed materials. The centre hosts around 100,000 visitors annually and relies on funds from a variety of sources including revenue from the sale of merchandise and local produce; ESS membership fees; volunteer contributions; and donations of members and visitors. The Rescue Centre provides a vital lifeline for adult turtles injured around the Zakynthos coast. Rehabilitated turtles have a chance of breeding again, thus improving the survival prospects for this endangered species. Research data gathered while treating injured turtles also adds to the international pool of knowledge which benefits all species of turtles worldwide.

The ESS also plays a critical role in lobbying the Greek Government to develop and enforce environmental legislation. For example, ESS has achieved speed, anchorage and fishing restrictions in the NMPZ; the banning of nocturnal light and noise at Laganas Bay to save energy and avoid disturbing the nocturnal nesting of turtles; warden patrols for the wider Bay area; the implementation of a strong forest policy and establishment of special forest fire services at all protected areas; increased funding of the forestry commission and environmental education; the enforcement of the laws in the National Forests; and clarification of land tenure rights.

To enrich and further support its activities, ESS has built and collaborates with a wider network of other local and international conservation associations (Table 9.3) to exchange knowledge, resources and collaboratively promote sustainability. For example, ESS works closely with Archelon, the Sea Turtle Protection Society of Greece and Global Vision International to bring in and educate volunteers to assist in the implementation of its programs.

Table 9.3: The collaborative network of ESS

Friends of the Ionian www.foi.org.uk	Sustainable tourism organisation working on all Ionian islands
Earth In Focus www.earthinfocus.com	A showcase for three up-and-coming photographers who all have a love of photography, travel and conservation.
Medasset www.medasset.gr	Greek conservation group working to protect sea turtles
Sea Turtles www.seaturtle.org	Track the progress of turtles fitted with radio tracking devices
Justzante www.justzante.co.uk	All you need to know about Zakynthos; user news & reviews
The NMPZ www.nmp-zak.org	The National Marine Park of Zakynthos
Archelon www.archelon.gr	Greek sea turtle conservation organisation that Nature World Travel and Earth Sea & Sky support at Gerakas
Euroturtle www.euroturtle.org	Turtle educational website

A significant amount of ESS' work depends on its volunteers. As such, ESS has built an international volunteer network to attract and connect participants from many different countries (http://earth-sea-sky-global.org/volunteer-opportu-nities). Its volunteer programme offers people the chance to take a holiday in Greece while simultaneously contributing to the future of the turtles. Volunteers can help in numerous activities such as: public education; beach clean-up; monitoring hatchlings; accompanying tourists at excursions; selling merchandise to raise funds; and working at the rescue and information centre.

In summary, the above analysis demonstrates the ability of organisations to create sustainable and shared value by expanding their value system to create a collaborative network of numerous stakeholders including NGO, locals, suppliers, partner and most importantly tourists. The role of tourists in sustainable tourism is of a critical importance, since without tourists' support and appropriate behaviour any sustainable activity could be undermined. To that end, the three organisations discussed are investing not only in tourists' environmental awareness and education, but also in empowering customers to become actively involved in conservation work. The latter is particularly important as studies in green consumer research show that the decision of a consumer to select and buy a sustainable product is influenced by their (social) learning, values, attitudes and lifestyle (Young et al., 2009; Sener & Hazer, 2008; Mair, 2011; McKercher & Prideaux, 2011).

■ Future Outlook

The economic crisis has severely impacted IEV organisations, as public funds and interest to support conservation work have been reduced significantly, while fundraising campaigns are finding it difficult to secure funds. The local tourism industry has also been negatively affected as tourists travel and spend less. To survive, local businesses tend to give higher priority to short term benefits over longer-term security and sustainability. As a result, the organisations are facing a major challenge to change the attitude and perceptions of locals, (potential) tourists and volunteers about the urgency to support conservation work during periods of the economic crisis.

To overcome these challenges, Mr Vardakastanis has started to exploit the tools and collaborative power of various social media tools (Table 9.4). Social media can reach a wide audience for increasing environmental awareness in order to motivate the active participation of people. Social media campaigns require minimal funding and, due to their popularity, international diffusion and social networking effects, they can:

- Disseminate information to a huge audience.
- Empower people to develop mass collaborative activities such as crowd funding for raising money, international petitions, recruiting of volunteers, global peer educations.
- Influence and amplify messages as a result of peer/social pressure (Sigala, 2010).

However, Mr Vardakastanis is not an expert on how to fully and effectively exploit the collaborative and networking power of social media. Thus, the volunteer work of social media experts will be required to expand and enrich the scope of activities of the organisation, while the support of all stakeholders (e.g. tourists, partners, locals) in creating, uploading, disseminating and critiquing user-generated-content will also be necessary for boosting the influence of the social media channels.

Table 9.4: Exploiting social media

www.thepetitionsite.com/2/the-illegal-hunting-of-migratory-birds-on-zakynthos-greece
   A petition website used by ESS in order to initiate and disseminate an online petition against illegal hunting of migratory birds

http://www.facebook.com/pages/Earth-Sea-Sky-Ionian-Nature-Conservation/120087021389714
   The Facebook profile and community of the three organisations

http://www.youtube.com/user/EARTHSEASKYorg
   The youtube channel of ESS for disseminating videos about their activities for raising awareness and educating the public

http://earth-sea-sky-global.org/about-us
   The blog of ESS used as a daily newsletter for supporting international public awareness and information

http://www.goabroad.com/providers/earth-sea-sky/programs/sea-turtle-and-wildlife-research-in-greece-55480
   GoAbroad.com is a leading international education and experiential travel resource. GoAbroad is also a worldwide volunteer network. ESS has used this network in order to initiate an international campaign for recruiting volunteers.

■ Summary and Conclusion

IEV, NWT and ESS represent three vertically integrated organisations that are funded and managed by Mr Vardakastani. The organisations are located in the NMPZ in Zakynthos, a fragile marine ecosystem where 80% of the endangered *Caretta Caretta* turtles living in the Mediterranean go to nest. The organisations have created and maintain a wide network of stakeholders (including locals, volunteers, suppliers and many other partners like NGOs) in order to develop collaborative activities that create shared and social value and benefits for all stakeholders. The current economic crisis has severely hit the organisations (fewer volunteers and fund raising opportunities). Given the popularity and the massive collaborative and networking capabilities of social media, the organisations are currently willing to further enrich and expand their sustainable practices by integrating and fully exploiting social media in their operations. However, the latter requires specialised knowledge and the support of many stakeholders, which is still to be gained.

9

■ Study Questions

1   Debate and give examples of why the creation of a collaborative network is important for achieving and supporting sustainability in tourism.

2   What practices have IEV, NWT and ESS developed for supporting sustainable tourism and creating shared value? Which stakeholders have they engaged with? What social benefits/value (economic, social and environmental) does each stakeholder get and what does each contribute through these collaborative activities?

3   Provide examples of how Mr Vardakastanis can exploit the power of crowdfunding for raising funds to support the conservation activities of his organisations. For example, how can websites such as www.spot.us, www.kickstarter.com and www.indiegogo.com be utilised?

4   Prepare a report analysing how Mr Vardakastanis can exploit social media for supporting the operations of his organisations (e.g. volunteer recruitment, sustainable promotion, raising environmental awareness and education). Your report should include the use of social media internally (i.e. how the organisation can develop and use its own social media tools, e.g. a blog) and externally (i.e. how the organisation can exploit existing social media such as Facebook). To better develop this report, investigate how the following organisations use social media: http://www.wwf.org/; http://www.conservation.org/; http://www.joinred.com/; www.oneplanetliving.org.

5   What advice would you give to Mr Vardakastanis to address the locals' persistence and priority towards short-term profit during this period of the economic crisis?

■ Useful Websites

www.lohas.com [accessed 26 October 2012]

www.natureworldtravel.com/marine_park.htm [accessed 12 November 2012]

www.relaxing-holidays.com [accessed 22 December 2012]

www.nmp-zak.org/ [accessed 22 December 2012]

www.greentreetransfers.com [accessed 22 December 2012]

■   References

Budeanu, A. (2005) 'Impacts and responsibilities for sustainable tourism: a tour operator's perspective', *Journal of Cleaner Production*, **13**, 89 – 97.

Choi, G., Parsa, H.G., Sigala, M. & Putrevu, S. (2009) 'Consumers' Environmental concerns and behaviours in the lodging industry: a comparison between Greece and the USA', *International Journal of Quality Assurance in Hospitality & Tourism*, **10** (2), 93 – 112.

Cronin, J.J., Smith, J.S., Gleim, M.R., Ramirez, E. & Martinez, J.D. (2011) 'Green marketing strategies: an examination of stakeholders and the opportunities they represent', *Journal of Academy of Marketing Science*, **39** (1), 158 – 174.

Fadeeva, Z. (2005) 'Translation of sustainability ideas in tourism networks: Some roles of cross-sectoral networks in change towards sustainable development', *Journal of Cleaner Production*, **13** (2), 175-189.

Fadeeva, Z. (2004) 'Development of the assessment framework for sustainability networking', *Journal of Cleaner Production*, **13**, 191 – 205.

Goldstein, N., Cialdini, R., & Griskevicious, V. (2008) 'A room with a viewpoint: using social norms to motivate environmental conservation in hotels', *Journal of Consumer Research*, **35**, 472 – 482.

Howe, J. (2008) *Crowdsourcing: Why the Power of the Crowd is Driving the Future of Business*, New York: Crown Business.

Kernel, P. (2005) 'Creating and implementing a model for sustainable development in tourism enterprises', *Journal of Cleaner Production*, **13**, 151 – 164.

Mair, J. (2011) 'Exploring air travellers' voluntary carbon-offsetting behavior', *Journal of Sustainable Tourism*, **19** (2), 215 — 230.

McKercher, B. & Prideaux, B. (2011) 'Are tourism impacts low on personal environmental agendas?', *Journal of Sustainable Tourism*, **19** (3), 325 – 345.

Moisander, J. (2007) 'Motivational complexity of green consumerism', *International Journal of Consumer Studies*, **31** (4), 404–409.

Morrison, A., Lynch, P. & Johns, N. (2004) 'International tourism networks', *International Journal of Contemporary Hospitality Management*, **16** (3), 197 - 202.

Porter, M. & Kramer, M.R. (2011) 'Creating shared value', *Harvard Business Review*, **89** (1/2), 62 – 77.

Relaxing Holidays (2012) 'Responsible tourism policy', retrieved from http://www.relaxing-holidays.com/responsible_tourism.htm on 15 February 2013.

Schwartz, K., Tapper, R. & Font, X. (2008) 'A sustainable supply chain management framework for tour operators', *Journal of Sustainable Tourism*, **16** (3), 298-314.

Sener, A. & Hazer, O. (2008) 'Values and sustainable consumption behaviour of women: a Turkish sample', *Sustainable Development*, **16** (5), 291– 300.

9

Sigala, M. (2008) 'A supply chain management approach for investigating the role of tour operators on sustainable tourism: the case of TUI', *Journal of Cleaner Production*, **16** (15), 1589-1599.

Sigala, M. (2010) 'The role of customers in sustainable supply chain management in tourism', paper presented at the Annual International Council for Hotel, Restaurant and Institutional Education (I-CHRIE) Convention, 28-31 July 2010, San Juan, Puerto Rico.

Sloan, P., Legrand, W. & Chen, J. (2013) *Sustainability in the Hospitality Industry: Principles of Sustainable Operations*, Oxon, UK: Routledge.

Tepelus, C. (2005) 'Aiming for sustainability in the tour operating business', *Journal of Cleaner production*, **13** (2), 7 – 107.

Terry, D.J., Michael A.H. & White, K.M. (1999) 'The theory of planned behaviour: Self-identity, social identity, and group norms', *British Journal of Social Psychology*, **38** (3), 225–44.

Tour Operators Initiative for Sustainable Tourism Development (2000) 'Good practice in sustainable tourism', paper presented at the World Travel Market, 15 November 2000, Paris.

Tour Operator Initiatives, TOI (2007) 'Integrating sustainable into the tour operators supply chain', retrieved from http://www.toinitative.org/index.php?id=53 on 23 August 2009.

Young, W., Hwang, K., McDonald, S. & Oates, C. (2009) 'Sustainable consumption: green consumer behavior when purchasing products', *Sustainable Development*, **18**, 20 – 31.

10 Back to the Roots: Agritourism in India

Nicole Häusler and **Dörte Kasüske,** *mas|contour – Sustainable Tourism Consulting & Communication*

Synopsis and Learning Outcomes

This case study introduces agritourism as an approach to tourism which may pave the way for sustainable development in rural areas. It provides a detailed discussion of the concept of agritourism, including the benefits, constraints and success factors involved, using the example of India, a country where 85% of the population depend on agriculture for their livelihood.

The Agri Tourism Development Corporation (ATDC) is an initiative which develops, actively promotes and encourages agritourism in the state of Maharashtra. The organisation aims to create sustainable livelihoods in rural areas by providing training, creating employment opportunities and linking tourism with agricultural production and related activities such as the manufacture of handicrafts. ATDC has established 113 Agri Tourism Centres across the state, which are run by local farmers and organisationally connected by ATDC. These Agri Tourism Centres serve predominantly domestic tourists from urban areas, who are provided with the opportunity to interact with rural villagers and farmers in order to experience authentic Indian agricultural traditions in unexploited natural environments.

This case study discusses the contributions of agritourism to farmers directly involved as well as to villagers indirectly affected by it. These contributions may range from economic benefits, education and awareness of the necessity to preserve natural resources to empowerment of marginalised community groups.

After completing this case study, learners will be able to:

1 Discuss advantages and disadvantages of implementing agritourism in rural areas.

2 Distinguish this approach from other tourism approaches.

3 Apply the concept of agritourism to specific cases and different contexts.

■   Background

In 2005, entrepreneur Pandurang Taware initiated a previously unknown business model in India, incorporating his professional experience and his family's farming background. Believing as he did that agritourism can contribute to poverty alleviation through the creation of sustainable livelihoods and the diversification of rural economies, he founded ATDC to promote and facilitate agricultural tourism in Maharashtra. The aim of this business model is to create employment opportunities and increase community income through small business development and local entrepreneurship by broadening the market base for local businesses (WTTC, 2012a). Mr Taware's vision is not purely based on business concepts; rather, he hopes that agritourism can revive an appreciation of Indian agricultural tradition and awareness of its importance within Indian society.

Figure 10.1: Agri Tourism Founder Pandurang Taware

ATDC acts as an umbrella organisation for the 113 regional Agri Tourism Centres, which are operated by local entrepreneurs and employees, and promotes their products in the target markets. Furthermore, the initiative provides training and capacity building for farmers, local guides and communities in the areas of small enterprise establishment and tourism product development. Since 2005, this free training has been provided to over 1,500 farmers (ATDC, 2012). In addition to offering these educational programmes, ATDC provides technical assistance and consulting services related to the preparation of project reports, sales and marketing activities (WTTC, 2012a).

The ATDC programme has various socioeconomic benefits:

- It generates additional income for the farmers, who have experienced a 25% income increase across the state.

- Activities in rural communities generate extra income for community members, such as retailers and service providers, who are not partners of ATDC. New tourism enterprises have been established by local community members under the guidance of ATDC as a result of new consumer market development.

- Awareness of local agricultural products has increased in urban communities, leading to direct sales from farmers to urban households.

- On-site employment opportunities have been created for members of farming families, eliminating the necessity to migrate to urban areas.

- Understanding of the value of agriculture and thus of the importance of maintaining agricultural lands has been improved through communication between urban Indians and rural people about the challenges of daily life.

Strong links between ATDC and the Maharashtra State Government have also led to improvements in the physical infrastructure (tourism accommodation facilities, road networks, electrical generating and distribution systems) in support of the Agri Tourism Centres (WTTC, 2012a).

Between 2007 and 2011, the offerings of Agri Tourism Centres across Maharashtra attracted over 200,000 visitors. Figure 10.2 shows that tourist arrivals in ATCs have increased significantly since 2007.

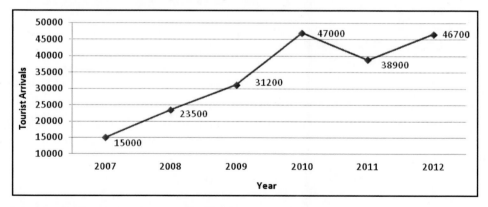

Figure 10.2: Tourist Arrivals in Agri Tourism Centres 2007–2012
Source: Based on data from Taware (2013), personal communication.

Domestic urban areas are the key markets, with 70% of all visitors originating from the city of Pune. The ATDC programme offers tourists participatory activities which provide an opportunity to experience local agricultural practices (horticulture, harvesting, beekeeping, dairying), rural ways of living and local culture (music, food, dances, handicrafts). Through its involvement with local community members, the programme promotes understanding and encourages urban Indians in particular to discover their roots. It also attracts international visitors with agritourism packages designed for independent and group travellers alike (ATDC, 2012).

■ Key Concepts

Many rural communities in developing countries are facing the challenge of finding appropriate income-generating activities because traditional agriculture-based rural economies do not offer sufficient employment opportunities. Young people in particular leave rural areas due to a lack of working opportunities. The tourism industry is a particularly suitable agent for **rural development** because it can have a number of positive effects (Häusler and Kotschi, 2011: 85):

- It rapidly creates long-term employment throughout different economic sectors, with significant direct effects on agriculture, construction and other local activities.

- It provides training and career development opportunities, thus serving as a springboard for the unemployed and unskilled workers to enter the labour market.

- It offers, especially to young people and women, good opportunities for livelihood diversification and helps alleviate rural poverty.

- It leads to the establishment of small and medium enterprises in the local community.

- It promotes local production (food, handicrafts), community pride, heritage and nature conservation.

- It helps to maintain local services and community facilities and thus to improve quality of life.

For these reasons, an increasing number of rural communities worldwide have turned to agritourism as an avenue for **poverty alleviation**. Agritourism is defined here as 'nearly any activity in which a visitor to the farm or other agricultural setting contemplates the farm landscape or participates in an agricultural process for recreation or leisure purposes' (Tew and Barbieri, 2012: 216). This includes outdoor activities such as daily visits (orchard tours, hayrides), recreational self-harvest, hunting and fishing for a fee, nature and wildlife observation, but also visits to special events and local festivals, educational activities and the purchase of agricultural goods.

Agritourism is widely regarded as a way to revitalise rural economies (Seong-Woo and Sou-Yeon, 2005), which can lead to a win-win situation for hosts and guests. Visitors are encouraged to experience agricultural life first-hand and farmers are enabled to diversify their activities while increasing the value of their products and property. Given this, the following activities should be integrated into the concept of agritourism (Häusler and Kotschi, 2011: 84):

■ Accommodation (traditional housing at the farm or at farm centres).

■ Board (providing local food and specialties).

■ Sale of local products, including food (packed tea, honey, dried fruits, herbs, fruit preserves, minor crops) as well as handicrafts made of natural materials (bamboo, rattan), painted pottery, carpets, hand-sewn clothes, traditional figurines and embroideries.

■ Renting of animals (horses, donkeys) for pleasure tours.

■ Creation of opportunities for hosts and guests to work together in the field to provide guests with local experiences.

■ Improvement of the knowledge of rural dwellers and their visitors about the protection and efficient utilisation of natural resources.

■ Development of new professional profiles (local tour guides, managers of travel circuits or accommodations).

■ Promotion of the sustainable use of biodiversity, including the valorisation of genetic heritage and development of the commodity chain for neglected medicinal and aromatic plant, grain and cereal species.

In essence, agritourism is about linking urban consumers (i.e. the tourists) with food producers so that small-scale regional farming can continue to be sustainable. Tourists who choose farm accommodations, rather than other kinds of accommodation facilities, look for a genuinely rural atmosphere where they can share the intimacy of their hosts' households, learn about traditional handicrafts and skills from their hosts, make friends (something almost forgotten in modern times) and, above all, enjoy homemade food. It is a strongly family-oriented recreational activity involving a journey back to the roots. The use of specific food labelling which identifies home-grown quality food and drink can help suppliers to establish markets for local products and can amount to a unique selling proposition when easily recognisable by tourists. Even if tourists do not stay overnight at the farm, local agriculture is linked in numerous ways to their activities. Local hotels and resorts can purchase food either directly from farmers or through local brokers, and visitors from nearby urban centres can be encouraged to purchase local produce and food products directly from the growers. In addition, farmers should be encouraged to use a variety of traditional, unique and 'exotic' agricultural products as a unique selling point for the region and appropriate training should be provided in this area.

Agritourism is not an easy approach to economic development and poverty alleviation because it requires business skills, an eagerness to serve others

10

(service-oriented thinking), and a strong commitment from community members and the local government. To achieve significant local **community involvement** in the rural tourism economy, intensive and professional training over a period of years is often a critical motivating factor. While the timing is good for the deployment of agritourism given the growing interest of consumers worldwide, poorly thought out approaches are unlikely to succeed. It is important for all stakeholders (government, the private sector and the communities) to take a long-term perspective. In particular, they must be aware of the challenges and barriers to the successful implementation of agritourism projects that farmers have to face (Häusler and Kotschi, 2011: 85):

- Limited knowledge of the tourism industry.
- Limited exposure to, understanding of and access to the markets.
- Little business experience.
- Lack of business and marketing strategies.
- Lack of available funding for marketing and promotion.
- Lack of service-oriented thinking among providers – passive attitude among locals.
- Insufficient training and education.
- Limited infrastructure.
- Inaccessibility of agritourism sites.

Given these assorted barriers, strategies for the implementation of agritourism must be adapted to the local context and capacities. Key elements of successful agritourism products, irrespective of the specific local conditions, include (Häusler and Kotschi, 2011: 88):

- Presenting a site-specific thematic story that includes a central theme or focus for visitors.
- Combining natural ecosystems and local communities in the visitors' exposure and experience.
- Demonstrating how people interact with nature.
- Educating visitors as well as villagers because education is a cornerstone of the experience.
- Authentic reflection of the reality of rural life patterns; what may be everyday business to the host community becomes extraordinary and unique to the visitors.
- Creating direct links between small-scale agriculture and the tourism experience.

It is of crucial importance to understand that the process of improving quality in accordance with pre-defined standards requires a close working relationship between all those involved in tourism in the destination, including government authorities, non-governmental organisations, private tourism businesses and small entrepreneurs (Häusler and Kotschi, 2011: 88).

■ Case Analysis

India, which is considered to be the world's largest democracy, has experienced significant economic growth in recent years. However, due to very uneven development, economic benefits continue to be limited to urban areas. Rural areas, where the majority of India's poor live, hardly benefit from the country's economic growth at all. In this light Selvaraj (2011: 6) states that a '[s]lowdown in agricultural growth and productivity, changing cropping patterns, increase in distress migration, changing consumption patterns, government policies favouring industrial houses, among others have seriously undermined the food and livelihood security of the poorer households'.

Moreover, a shift in economic structures has been observed. After India gained independence in 1947, agriculture contributed about 55% to the national GDP (Bhalla, 2008: 3). By 2010, this contribution had fallen to only 19% of the national GDP (World Bank, 2012). With 58% of the rural population still depending on agriculture as their main source of income (UNDP, 2013), this sector is not merely a business but rather the 'True Culture of India' and the backbone of its economy.

Crop yields have slowed due to uncertain climatic conditions and the fact that there exists no minimum support price guarantee. These changes have altered the forms and practices of farming operation. Farmers are looking beyond traditional farming by selling their products to a wholesaler to generate income through various forms of direct on-farm marketing and farm-based non-agricultural business.

Tourism has contributed greatly to the increase of prosperity in India. In 2011, the tourism sector directly and indirectly contributed 6.4% to India's GDP (WTTC, 2012b). Domestic tourism is of exceptional importance for the industry. In view of over 850 million domestic trips taken in 2011, the 6.29 million recorded arrivals of international tourists pale in comparison, but it must also be noted that foreign exchange earnings from tourism contributed €12.92 billion to India's national income in that year (MoT, 2012). Furthermore, the tourism industry created 39.4 million direct and indirect jobs in 2011, representing 7.9% of total employment. Capital investment in the travel and tourism industry was €17.83 billion in 2011 and is expected to increase by 7.5% per annum over the next ten years (WTTC, 2012b).

10

Domestic tourism has also shown greater buoyancy and resilience than arrivals by international travellers. Over the last 15 years, domestic tourism has grown by over 300 million trips, from 63 million in 1990 to 367 million in 2005, representing an annual growth of 20%. With regard to the industry's long-term growth, the World Travel and Tourism Council has rated India as one of the five fastest-growing tourism economies in the world (WTTC, 2012b).

Maharashtra is the third-largest and the second most populous state in India. It is located on the west coast of India, with a 720-km coastline along the lush green Konkan region. The state abounds in tourist attractions, which include lively metropolises such as Mumbai and Pune, historic monuments such as ancient caves, temples and forts, the natural beauty of unspoilt beaches, dense forests, several wildlife sanctuaries and nature parks and cultural richness in the form of pilgrimage centres, numerous festivals and traditional arts and culture (Gopal et al., 2008: 513). In 2011, 55 million domestic trips and 4.8 million international tourist arrivals to the state were recorded. Maharashtra ranks fifth among India's states in terms of domestic tourist arrivals and first in terms of international tourist arrivals (MoT, 2012).

When Mr Taware, founder of ATDC, started to develop his new business idea of linking tourism and agriculture, he conducted a consumer survey in Pune with a sample size of 2,440. The results of the survey showed that connections between Pune's urban population and the surrounding rural areas were quite weak: 35% of the urban population did not have any relatives in the villages; 43% had never visited or stayed in rural communities; and 57% had never visited a dairy farm. According to Mr Taware, these results confirmed the need to start a pilot project because the figures clearly showed that there were a huge number of urban Indians who had never experienced rural life. ATDC's mission statement reflects the aims of the enterprise:

'To promote agriculture tourism to achieve income, employment and economic stability in rural communities in India. To help boosting a range of activities, services and amenities provided by farmers and rural people to attract urban tourists to their area, thus providing opportunity to urban people to get back to the rural roots' (Gopal et al., 2008: 518).

After a successful two-year pilot phase at one farm, ATDC decided to expand its programme to other villages and farmers throughout the state of Maharashtra. In the second phase, farmers from various villages were selected to participate in the programme and over 250 farmers received capacity-building training in the area of agritourism. To address challenges and barriers to the successful implementation of agritourism, ATDC provided associated farmers with support on the following issues:

■ Preparation of ATDC project reports and business plans for all agricultural farms applying for the programme.

■ Assistance in facilitating financial support from national banks, institutes and government agencies to build agritourism facilities and infrastructure (accommodation, sanitation, access roads).

■ Sales and marketing support.

■ Coordination of tours from urban areas to the farms.

ATDC's activities in the area of product development include farm tours, tractor and bullock cart rides, visits to farms which produce fruit (grapes, mangos) and by-products and farms which raise birds and other animals (poultry, dairy cattle, goats) (see Figure 10.3). Visitors can also visit local facilities such as *gram panchayat*[1] village offices and schools, village fairs and markets, a sugar factory, milk collection centres and some of the oldest religious temples and museums in Maharashtra. Educational programmes are also offered to the visitors on such topics as how to grow crops and operate fruit plantations, the nutritional value of different fruits, how to take care of cattle, nature education, domestic animals and different types of trees, goat and cow milking, honey making, silk making, jaggery making and rural games, watching domestic animals, clay moulding, painting natural scenes and tree climbing. The various activities, which are developed by local community members assisted by ATDC, keep the visitors quite busy, even at remote farms in the Indian countryside.

Figure 10.3: Bullock cart rides provided by farmers

1   Gram panchayats consist of 7 to 17 members, who are elected from the wards of the village.

In the evenings, rural Maharashtra folk dances and folk song programmes, winter campfires and family games are organised. The food served is Maharashtrian style and includes fresh green vegetables. Basic accommodation, which is built using local materials, is provided in neat and clean rooms in vernacular architectural style and design at the farm.

According to Gopal et al. (2008: 515), three important factors contribute to the success of agritourism:

- **Farmers**: Most farmers welcome visitors warmly and without any commercial motives. The farming families entertain their guests while entertaining themselves, filling all the service gaps in the process. This makes them natural businesspeople and creates the experience of hospitality in its purest sense.

- **Villages**: Because many of the villages are located far from the cities, they lack urban facilities. However, the locations are rich in natural resources; these natural resources themselves are unique-selling-propositions for the farmers.

- **Geographic areas**: Each area is unique, thus representing a competitive advantage for rural people and adding to the attraction of the urban population.

According to a survey (ATDC, 2012), ATDC has achieved a number of positive results in the seven years since its foundation:

- The lives of the farmers have changed considerably as a result of the ATDC destination venture. They do not only gain additional income but are especially proud to be able to manage this new business in a successful way.

- Most of the farmers who cooperate with ATDC have become entrepreneurs.

- On average, 33% of the farmers' income has been generated by agritourism.

- The sale of agritourism products at the Agri Tourism Centre (ATCs) has generated a gross annual income of approx. €4,270 per farm.

- 442 rural community members have found employment at ATCs (not including farmers' family members).

- On average, each ATC has created direct and indirect employment for eight people in the rural areas of Maharashtra.

- These people have been trained soft skills which enable them to provide customer service and market their products.

- Participation in agritourism activities has raised the farmers' self-esteem.

- Other villagers such as women's self-help groups, local artisans and artists have experienced significant economic benefits as well.

- Agritourism in Maharashtra has had a positive effect on communities in drought-prone areas which had previously exhibited rising suicide rates.

- Local farmers believe that the natural environment has benefited from the ATDC initiative.

- Since 2005, the ATDC destinations have hosted over 25,300 tourists from urban cities every year.
- The existing natural resources are utilised efficiently.

ATDC also addresses the challenges involved in such a tourism concept, including:

- Risk of overexploitation of natural resources.
- Uncertain demand for agritourism because it competes with other forms of tourism.
- Provision and maintenance of hygienic conditions at ATDC destinations.
- Insufficient government support.
- Follow-up training for the farmers.
- Large-scale power cuts.
- Accessibility and approachability of the area with respect to basic facilities (medical facilities, transport facilities, availability of water).

According to Gopal et. al (2008: 520), the success or failure of any Agri Tourism Centre ultimately depends on the involvement of the farmers' family members, the local community and the deep-rooted networking requirements at both the local and state levels. Indeed, networking is one of the key issues in making Indian agritourism sustainable in the long run.

Based on its own past experiences, ATDC states that for an agritourism venture to be successful, the following important conditions must be fulfilled:

1 Potential tourists must be offered a complete tourism package. This requires the participation of all businesses in the area and for local government bodies to initiate activities such as beautification campaigns and sponsorship of special events that tie in with local tourist attractions.

2 Successful tourism promotion and development requires good community leadership by open-minded and enthusiastic individuals from local government, community groups, the business community and non-profit organisations such as the chambers of commerce and convention and visitor bureaus.

3 Local government must actively participate and provide support in the following areas: funding for tourism development and promotion; the creation and maintenance of the infrastructure necessary for tourism; the zoning and maintenance of the community so that it looks clean and appealing to tourists, and the provision of educational support to farmers.

10

■ Future Outlook

Agritourism development in the rural areas of Maharashtra is still at a very early stage, and a variety of opportunities exist for the state to improve its agritourism products. Although the state government has shown little initiative so far, agritourism has been successfully initiated thanks to the farmers' efforts. According to Gopal et al. (2008: 521), the following framework conditions must be met for the successful promotion of agritourism to achieve business sustainability in the long run:

1 *Sufficient funding for tourism development:* Most rural communities depend on public funding, which is very often insufficient to cover all of the communities' needs. Private funding is unavailable in most cases because local people do not have sufficient income to invest. Therefore, it is necessary to explore other sources of funding and assistance.

2 *Strategic planning:* Planning is fundamental to the efficient and effective use of resources and funding, especially in rural areas where such factors are limited. Good planning of tourism development and promotion can help develop and support local businesses connected to tourism and should be integrated into a community's overall economic strategy because of the interdependence of the community and key aspects of tourism development and promotion. Hence, tourism planning requires the involvement of various stakeholders in the community.

3 *Coordination and cooperation between businesspersons and local leadership:* For tourism development and planning to be successful, coordination and cooperation between local government and entrepreneurs is crucial. While strong personal networks are typical strengths of rural communities, coordination and cooperation between local government and the business community are not always easily achieved, if at all.

4 *Coordination and cooperation between rural tourism entrepreneurs:* The very nature of tourism requires that different types of businesses such as shops, accommodation facilities, restaurants and tourist attractions work together to create the overall tourist experience. These complex supply chain relationships, and the performance of individual firms, can be improved through the creation of formal and informal networks. Tourism networks allow for standardised yet high-quality business management, which small enterprises do not have, to improve strategic planning and tactical decision-making on issues such as pricing, product differentiation and yield management. Tourism networks can also substantially improve the performance of small tourism businesses by transforming their sometimes scattered products into a one-stop shop solution to sell a wide variety of functionally interrelated tourism products.

5 *Information and technical assistance concerning tourism development and promotion*: The provision and sharing of different types of information relating to tourism development and promotion are particularly important to agritourism development because small communities usually cannot afford to hire experts. The role of the networks discussed above is also of utmost importance in this regard.

6 *Widespread community support for tourism development:* Community support for tourism development and the attitudes and hospitality of local tourism workers are crucial for successful tourism projects. Whole community efforts are required in managing and marketing tourism because it is the image of the community as a whole, rather than that of single attractions, which must be marketed.

■ Summary and Conclusion

The Agri Tourism Development Corporation benefits local communities in that it creates alternative livelihoods for the rural population, thus encouraging community members to remain in or return to their home community. ATDC's focus is on providing training and employment for local youth at Agri Tourism Centres to give them the opportunity to earn their livelihood in the community and to start their own agricultural tourism business. Women in particular receive special support in the form of service contracts for food preparation at the associated tourism centres.

For agritourism to succeed, it is imperative that the tourists have:

■ *Something to see*: Animals, birds, farms, village culture, traditional dress, festivals.

■ *Something to do*: Participation in agricultural operations, riding camels and buffalo, cooking and participating in rural games (Gilli Danda, Gotti, Marbles).

■ *Something to buy*: Rural handicrafts, dress materials, farm gate-fresh processed food.

Although ATDC has accomplished various achievements in the past, additional requirements have to be met to ensure business sustainability in the long run. Such requirements include appropriate funding for development activities, strategic planning, cooperation among stakeholders, the provision of information, technical advice and widespread support for local farmers and rural communities to help them get involved in agritourism activities.

10

■   **Study Questions**

1   Apart from economic benefits, how can agritourism contribute to sustainability and the well-being of rural communities?

2   Do you know of any agritourism products in your country? How do they differ from agritourism products in Maharashtra in terms of aims, framework conditions and demand and supply? Do you see any similarities?

3   Suggest an agenda for a two-day visit to a farm in Maharashtra. Which elements should be included and why?

4   What are some of the challenges faced by ATDC? Develop strategies for overcoming three of the challenges you have identified.

■   **References**

ATDC (Agri Tourism Development Corporation) (2012) 'Agri Tourism Sector Study Report', [Powerpoint Presentation].

Bhalla, S. (2008) 'Indian Economic Growth 1950–2008: Facts & Beliefs, Puzzles & Policies', retrieved from http://oxusinvestments.com/files/pdf/110IndianEconomicGrowth 1950-2008.pdf on 15 November 2012.

Gopal, R., Varma, S. & Gopinathan, R. (2008) 'Rural Tourism Development: Constraints and Possibilities with a special reference to Agri Tourism. A Case Study on Agri Tourism Destination – Malegoan Village, Taluka Baramati, District Pune, Maharashtra', retrieved from http://dspace.iimk.ac.in/bitstream/2259/596/1/512-523.pdf on 15 November 2012.

Häusler, N. & Kotschi, J. (2011) 'Agro-ecotourism', in L. Waldmueller (ed.) *Training of Trainers. Sourcebook on Conservation and Management of Agrobiodiversity in the People's Republic of China*, Beijing: Deutsche Gesellschaft für Internationale Zusammenarbeit (GIZ), pp. 84–88.

Häusler, N. (2011) 'Same same but different – concepts of tourism dimensions', *Rural 21*, **4**, 16.

MoT (Ministry of Tourism of India) (2012) 'India Tourism Statistics at a Glance 2011', retrieved from http://tourism.gov.in/writereaddata/CMSPagePicture/file/marketresearch/INDIATOURISMSTATICS%28ENGLISH%29.pdf on 15 November 2012.

Seong-Woo, L. & Sou-Yeon, N. (2005) 'Agro-Tourism as a Rural Development Strategy in Korea', *Journal of Rural Development*, **29** (6), 67–83.

Selvaraj, A. (2011) 'An Economic Introspection of Rural-Urban Livelihoods in India', retrieved from http://www.indialabourstat.com/article/29/anitha/fulltext.pdf on 28 January 2013.

Taware, P. (2013) Personal Communication.

Tew, C. & Barbieri, C. (2012) 'The perceived benefits of agritourism: The provider's perspective', *Tourism Management*, **33** (1), 215–224.

UNDP (2013) 'Greening Rural Development in India, Volume 1', retrieved from http://www.undp.org/content/dam/india/docs/EnE/greening-rural-development-in-india.pdf on 28 January 2013.

World Bank (2012) 'India at a Glance', retrieved from http://devdata.worldbank.org/AAG/ind_aag.pdf on 15 November 2012.

WTTC (World Travel & Tourism Council) (2012a) 'Report on Community Benefit Award Finalist 2011: Case Study: Tourism for Tomorrow Awards 2012', retrieved from http://www.wttc.org/site_media/uploads/downloads/Agri_Tourism_Development_Corporation.pdf on 15 November 2012.

WTTC (World Travel & Tourism Council) (2012b) 'Travel and Tourism Economic Impact 2012 India', retrieved from http://www.wttc.org/site_media/uploads/downloads/india2012.pdf on 15 November 2012.

10

11 Namibia's Communal Conservancy Tourism Sector

Dr. Joram Ndlovu, *University of KwaZulu-Natal*

Synopsis and Learning Outcomes

The purpose of this case study is to provide insights into the strategies undertaken by the Namibian Government to use tourism as an incentive for local communities to coexist with wildlife, including predators. Its relevance is based on the types of incentives used and the level of stakeholders' participation. The case study highlights the constitutive role of policy and policy alignment in community-based tourism programmes. Three core issues are discussed, namely: devolution of rights over wildlife and tourism to communities; establishment of tourism joint ventures; and the impacts of tourism at local, national, regional and international levels. To understand the context of sustainable tourism development, the case study examines theories relevant to the support and sustenance of tourism within local community contexts. Such theories include common property resource theory and practice, social exchange theory, social representations theory and community participation theory. Muller's (1994, cited in Sharpley & Telfer, 2002) 'Magic Pentagon of Sustainable Tourism Development and Equity' theory are also used to put the case into perspective (*see* Giaoutzi & Nijkamp, 2006). The case highlights the achievements of communal conservancies, which include:

- Empowering communities to make their own decisions regarding sustainable utilisation of their natural and cultural assets.

- Providing rights and tenure over natural resources through the promulgation of a tourism policy to enable communities to earn an income and other related direct or indirect benefits.

- The accruing benefits from the allocation of hunting quotas to local communities and other commercial products derived from community forests.

- The exponential growth of conservancies which has increased opportunities for employment, training, capacity building and other economic prospects for the locals.

- Helping in tackling HIV issues during community gatherings by educating communities about the AIDS pandemic.

After studying the case study, learners should be able to:

1   Evaluate the role of tourism as both a conservation and development tool in Namibia, particularly in relation to wildlife conservation and employment creation in communities where few alternative job opportunities exist.

2   Assess the extent to which strong incentives can redirect community efforts to manage their natural resources in a sustainable manner to enhance their livelihoods.

3   Discuss ways in which communities can capitalise on rapidly growing global tourism demands to boost tourism revenues and diversify their rural livelihoods away from primary traditional subsistence farming.

4   Provide insights with regard to benefit sharing and make feasible recommendations on tourism governance in the conservancy tourism sector.

■ Background

The Republic of Namibia's constitution stipulates in article 95 (1) on the environment and policies (*see* http://www.environment-namibia.net/constitution.html), the importance of promotion and maintenance of the welfare of the people of Namibia through sustainable utilisation of natural resources for the benefits of all Namibians (Government of Namibia, 1990:36). As a result, tourism has been used such that sustainable utilisation of natural resources can benefit the local community in Namibia. Namibia has managed to enhance its tourism offering through a mix of natural resources conservation and development. With its diverse landscapes, the 'big-five', and rich cultures, the country has managed to support a mix of land conservation models, including communal conservancies. In order to achieve this, the Government has incorporated the concept of environmental protection into its constitution to facilitate the implementation of Human Wild Life Conflict (HWLC) (see Appendix 1) and Community Based Natural Resources Management programme (CBNRM) (see Appendix 2) policies.

In 1995 the Government developed and approved a policy for the creation of community-level conservancies. The following year in 1996, the Nature Conservation Amendment Act Number 5 amended the Nature conservation Ordinance of 1975 so that residents of communal areas could gain the same rights over wildlife and tourism as commercial farmers. The Act makes the formation of a conservancy a condition for giving rights over game and tourism to communal area residents of a certain territory. A conservancy on communal land can be defined as "a community or group of communities within a defined geographical area who jointly manage, conserve and utilise the wildlife and other natural resources within the defined area" (Jones, 1995). The map in Figure 11.1 shows the landscape and the area of conservancies in Namibia.

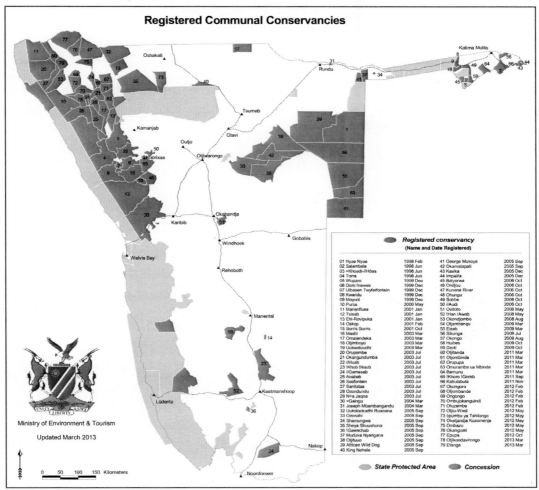

Figure 11.1: Namibia-Area of conservation. *Source:* NACSO, 2010

In the past, local communities were not involved in the planning and development of tourism on their communal lands (Ashley, 1999), which tended to shift tourism benefits to investors. Over the past 20 years, the CRNRM programme has grown dramatically and achieved its wildlife conservation and rural development objectives. The preservation of large, unfenced areas of land has managed to restore natural wildlife corridors. In order to restore and expand the range of wildlife populations, the Government of Namibia embarked on a deliberate programme to translocate rare and endangered species from national parks to communal conservancies (MET, 2010). Having started with 13% of communal land area under conservation management in 1998, conservancies now cover over 41.8% of communal land in Namibia, which is 16.1% of the total land area. Conservancies involve 59 communities (with an additional 30 communities in the process of establishing conservancies), and generate over N$45.8 million annually (NACSO, 2010). Figure11.2 shows the growth of conservancies in terms of their cash income, non-cash income and income from CBNRM activities.

N$ (million)

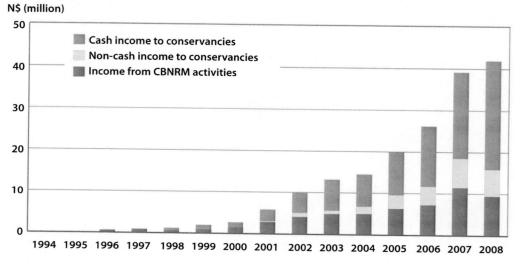

Figure 11.2: Income to conservancies and from CBNRM activities. *Source:* NACSO, 2010

The communal conservancy tourism sector has become a dynamic part of the national tourism industry, and contributes both direct and indirect benefits to local communities. To ensure continued growth in communal conservancies, the private sector has invested thousands of dollars (US$) in the accommodation sector. With an average of 1,400 bed nights per month, the current lodges are creating much needed employment in remote rural areas where few other job opportunities exist. Tourism is the fourth largest income generator in Namibia with approximately 234,300 people benefiting from the conservancies and about 10,000 jobs created. By the end of 2010, greater focus was placed on building capacities for managing conservancy finances, with an emphasis on implementing formal systems and providing regular feedback to members. A total of 27 conservancies have established financial sustainability plans which guide conservancy planning and management. A total of 619 conservancy management jobs existed in 2010, the majority of which were entirely funded by the conservancies themselves. The Government of the Republic of Namibia has designated tourism as a priority area for growth and development through its *Vision 2030* published in 2004 (see http://www.npc.gov.na/vision/vision_2030bgd.htm), *National Development Plan*

III published in 2011, and its *National Poverty Alleviation Strategy for 2009-2013* (*see* http://www.npc.gov.na/npc/ndp3info.html). To achieve this broad strategy, the Government, with the assistance of the private sector, non-governmental organisations (NGOs) and other stakeholders, has directd funding and resources to conservancies in order to diversify rural livelihoods and supplement subsistence agricultural production.

■ Key Concepts

In designing new policies and legislation, Namibian government officials were able to draw upon important advances in **Common Property Resource Theory and Practice (CPRTP)** (Pretty, 2003; Jones & Murphree, 2004; Jones, 2005) which give rise to devolving proprietorship over common-pool resources, such as wildlife, to a group of individuals on land owned by the State (Shackleton *et al.*, 2002; Barnes *et al.*, 2001; Tacconi, 2007). CPRTP had a significant influence on the current CBNRM program in Namibia (Sebele, 2010) since it is premised on the notion that the **community** should have a defined membership, a set of agreed operating and resource use rules, the ability to monitor compliance with rules and enforce them, a defined area in which the resource is 'owned' and managed, as well as legitimacy from the resource users and from the State (Barnes *et al.*, 2001; Ashley, 2000; Murphy & Roe, 2004). This is a form of decentralisation of power and authority. The development of CBNRM policy and legislation provides for rights over wildlife and tourism to be given to communal area residents who form a 'conservancy', thereby transferring rights, power, authority and resources to institutions that represent and are accountable to local people (Trick, 2000; Barnes *et al.*, 2002; Ribot, 2004; Murphree, 2004).

This principle is also a good illustration of **Social Exchange Theory (SET)** which states that residents are likely to have a positive attitude towards tourism as long as the perceived benefits exceed the perceived costs (Murphy & Murphy, 2004). Related studies on residents' attitudes towards tourism development have mainly been focused on the economic front, rather than the social aspects (Jones, 2003; Matose, 2004: Sebele, 2010). Whilst it is acknowledged that tourism can be used as a tool for development, studies tend to ignore fundamental issues such as social norms, values and beliefs of local communities towards tourism, which are variables that can influence the direction of development (Ashley, 1999; Long & Jones, 2004; Jones, 2005). In order to understand these variables and their impact on tourism (Faulkner & Tideswell, 1997), it is useful to use **Social Representations Theory (SRT)** to explain how the attitudes of individuals and residents can be managed for a common goal (Murphy & Murphy, 2004).

Other researchers (e.g. Gächter & Fehr, 1999; McGehee & Santos, 2005; McIntosh & Zahra, 2007) have used **Equity and Community Participation**

11

Theories. The former argues that communities are likely to bring about the desired transformation if their desires, either as a group or individually, are correlated to the perception of equity, fairness and justice practiced by management. This is premised on the notion that the greater the individual's or group's perception of fairness, the higher the motivation level, and vice versa. In evaluating fairness, employees compare the task input (in terms of contribution) to outcome (in terms of compensation) and compare this ratio with that of another peer of equal cadre/category. In this way, community participation is deeply ideological and reflects beliefs about bureaucratisation, centralisation, remoteness and the rigidity of the state (Midgley *et al.*, 1996).

Community participation embraces dynamism on how conflicting interests are resolved for the general welfare of a group. Similarly, Muller (1994, cited in Sharpley & Telfer, 2002) in his Magic Pentagon of Sustainable Tourism cautions that sustainable tourism should ensure economic health, satisfaction of guests, healthy culture, protection of resources and wellbeing of locals. The magic pentagon has five pillars. It propagates for the preservation of the unspoilt nature and environment by capitalising on environmental protection. The aim of tourism is to provide lasting experiences to the target audience. Therefore, tourism should result in optimum guest satisfaction and repeat visitation. Tourism should ensure a healthy culture for the locals by maintaining the subjective wellbeing of the locals. Destinations should not solely depend on tourism but tourism should supplement the economy appropriately and involve locals in tourism development activities. The magic pentagon of sustainable tourism development cautions that destinations should minimise the negative effects of tourism on the environment and avoid the pitfalls of economic imperatives where tourism becomes a panacea for all the country' ills. Therefore tourism development should be limited to what is feasible and not extended to what is considered by some to be desirable. Pursuing active planning and land use policy should take care of the natural resources and limit development to planned targets.

Drawing on the lessons above, it can be concluded that for tourism to be sustainable, local communities should fully participate in tourism development in order to instil a sense of ownership and increase opportunities for personal benefits and improved livelihoods for the locals.

■ Case Analysis

Both before and since achieving independence in 1990, Namibia has largely depended on the extraction of mineral resources for growth and development. Of late, however, the Government has faced the challenge of high unemployment. During the war of liberation between the South African administration and

SWAPO (South West People Organisation), wild animals were hunted to near extinction. The previous regime had given white farmers exclusive rights over the management of wildlife resources. Following independence, the major task faced by the new government of Namibia was to devise strategies for reducing human-wildlife conflict, managing wildlife and increasing the benefits thereof. The tourism sector has only recently been recognised as a key factor in achieving these goals through the Broad Based Economic Empowerment programme (BBEE) and a tourism-focused initiative meant to reduce the persistent high unemployment rate among the unskilled youth, called the Targeted Intervention Programme for Employment and Economic Growth (TIPEEG) (*see* http://www.npc.gov.na/publications/TIPEEG.pdf). The main goals of TIPEEG are employment creation, attracting investment, and increasing economic growth and capacity building.

In addition to these initiatives, a critical development for the stimulation of tourism in rural areas of Namibia was the establishment of wildlife conservancies, which have been promoted through CBNRM (Tacconi, 2007). In the early 1990s the idea of CBNRM emerged as a result of the success of CAMPFIRE (Communal Areas Management Programme For Indigenous Resources) in Zimbabwe and the CBNRM programme in Botswana (Sebele, 2010). The introduction of a holistic tourism policy in 1996 by the Namibian Ministry of Environment and Tourism (*see* http://www.namibweb.com/tourpolicy.htm) signalled a change in the approach to wildlife management. The policy, in line with the country's Vision 2030, pursued the idea of devolving authority over wildlife and tourism to local communities themselves. This initiative gave rise to the present conservancy phenomenon (see http://www.nacso.org.na/dwnlds/MET_policy_on_CBT_development.pdf) which seeks to embrace the opportunities for local communities to manage their wildlife resources in a sustainable manner (Barnes *et al.*, 2001; Sebele, 2010). Through this model, the Government of Namibia has created a framework for partnering successfully with local people to conserve their abundant natural resources while realising substantive economic benefits (Shackleton *et al.*, 2002) to improve their livelihoods, which other developing countries can exploit as a best-practice example (Barnes *et al.*, 2001).

The formation of a conservancy involves a participatory process whereby the majority of people in the area are required to agree with the concept. Based on the majority view, a constitution is then drawn up to provide guidelines for annual meetings as well as to establish boundary management committees and their functions. Mainly, the Management committee creates and maintains membership lists, develops game management plans, creates dispute resolution mechanisms, arranges and holds annual meetings, and report to conservancy members. Once approved by the Ministry of Environment and Tourism (MET), conservancies are gazetted (Ashley, 1999). The CBNRM programme has shifted

11

the natural resources management function away from the state and has allocated the responsibilities and benefits of managing the conservancy to local communities (Shackleton *et al.*, 2002; Barnes *et al.*, 2001). Conservancies are intended to protect wildlife and its habitat. To this end, technical assistance is provided by MET and NGOs in managing the conservancy. As rights over wildlife do not imply unlimited hunting, the MET sets quotas for hunting such that wildlife populations remain stable. Game wardens from the community are employed by the conservancy to patrol and deter poachers, and sometimes to track them down and arrest them with assistance from MET Rangers, as well as assisting the MET to monitor wildlife numbers during annual game counts (MET, 2010).

Conservancies also have rights over tourism operations, management and control of resources (Tacconi, 2007). When an investor wants to open a lodge in a conservancy area, the investor has to sign a JV (joint venture) agreement with the community from which, ideally, both sides benefit; the conservancy can share a percentage of the income from the lodge as well as ensuring that the local community is prioritised regarding job opportunities The communal conservancy strategy seeks to capitalise on rapidly growing global demands for authentic attractions, as well as conservation and protection of wildlife and cultural heritage resources. As a result, the Namibian Government has used tourism as both a conservation and development tool.

While the CBNRM is based on the principle of equitable distribution of natural resources and benefits, not all conservancies can yield benefits, not all JVs are profitable and not all benefits are equally distributed. Even though this form of tourism is meant to contribute to poverty alleviation, improve quality of life and ensure the empowerment of local people, most beneficiaries tend to be those holding positions of influence. Community members are more concerned about benefit sharing than the cost of bringing tourists to the destination. Most of the community members are illiterate and they do not have adequate skills for managing tourism facilities. The failure by conservancy members to participate meaningfully in decision making has left them as spectators, leaving all decisions to be taken by the conservancy management. Despite the fact that locals are involved in CBTEs, the current levels of community members' management skills do not encourage entrepreneurship. Furthermore, local communities are incapacitated due to a lack of resources for both marketing and product development. Considering the way in which CBT is isolated from mainstream tourism, and tourist perceptions that CBT products are of inferior quality, community benefits are marginal at the present time. Most of the CBT products are not demand-driven which has an effect on the number of tourists visiting some conservancies. To increase community benefits, target markets have to be identified followed by aggressive marketing of these products.

Even though NGOs and other partner organisations have helped in financing community projects in Namibia, community dynamics tend to hamper progress. Among the most noticeable challenges is the remoteness of CBTEs which limits local communities from readily showcasing their unique cultural handicrafts and other artefacts. Improving this situation may require capitalisation, yet it is extremely expensive to borrow money from financial institutions due to high interest rates. While communities could use their land as collateral, this may pose a high risk to the public resource. Therefore the management of tourism expectations and local community perceptions has become a big challenge for investors. On one hand the Government expects tourism to be the answer to all social ills facing rural communities. On the other hand local communities seem to believe that tourism operators are short changing them in dividends. While the existing literature on CBT development in Namibia has focused on the expectations of government, NGOs, business investors, donors and tourists, limited information is available on local community perceptions towards CBT development. Lack of validated case studies on community based tourism has hampered the understanding of local community needs with regard to tourism development in Namibia. Some scholars have advocated the determination of local community perceptions and values as a prerequisite for establishing a successful and sustainable tourism sector (Jones & Luipert, 2002; Sebele, 2010; Ndlovu *et al.*, 2011).

Only registered members of the conservancy are eligible to receive dividends from joint-venture agreements, thereby excluding 'other' members of the community. Sometimes it is confusing to know who gets the benefits, since this aspect is left to the conservancies to define through their constitutional processes. The policy requires that membership is based on those who signed the registration form and there is no membership card given, which further complicates the benefit distribution process. Of note is the evident lack of equitable income distribution to families affected by HIV/AIDS. There is often a misconception that if an individual lives within a conservancy boundary, the individual automatically becomes a conservancy member. Despite having registered relatively large incomes and pay-outs, high levels of poverty, unemployment, unequal distribution of income, unskilled labour and alcohol abuse continue to affect local community conservancies. Considering that in some conservancies there are few opportunities for employment, the conservancies remain the sole source of livelihood.

The local community's level of participation in tourism planning and development is limited to conservancy committee members which leaves the decision-making process to a few individuals. A strong participatory approach can enhance benefit distribution plans and give conservancy members an opportunity to fully participate in decisions to do with revenue distribution. In addition, the exclusion of conservancy members from the decision making body has resulted in those professionally involved in tourism planning and development (government, NGOs, donors and tourism business investors) being viewed as the only experts guiding tourism development in Namibia with little input from the community at large. As a result, infrastructure development often fails to cater for local communities' basic physiological needs such as water, food, shelter and clothing. For example, there is no programme in place to provide decent housing for local people or to build permanent structures from conservancy funds.

Participation comes in different forms; people can be encouraged to develop tourism enterprises through incentives which enable them to benefit from tourism while conserving wildlife and natural resources (NACSO, 2010). This shows that tourism development can work hand-in-hand with environmental conservation but, for it to be realistic, people must be consulted and their ideas must be included in tourism planning and legislation. In cases where large businesses operate on communal land, local residents should be involved and must reap a portion of the benefits. The success of tourism is premised on increased representation of communities in tourism organisations with the aim of prioritising community interests in planning and giving people choice as to how they want to run tourism ventures. To achieve this, revenue-sharing and partnership matrices should be based on the maximum number of people who stand to benefit from the venture. The model on which conservancies are developed in Namibia has in many ways given people rights over the use of natural resources such as wildlife and tourism sites. However, this process is not cheap as it requires investment in communal areas, good tourism planning, training of local staff and marketing and promotion of tourism in the destination. Because people in rural areas have no means of raising capital, commercial tourism ventures should set-up local funds which can be used to help people in rural areas plan and start new activities. Since rural tourism is different from mainstream tourism, continued promotion of community-based tourism products needs to be carefully coordinated. This should be supported by unrelenting communication between communities, the government, NGOs and the private sector in helping to sustain conservancies.

■ Future Outlook

Tourism conservancies have been used as a strategy for sustainable utilisation of natural resources for the benefit of rural communities in Namibia. The success of this programme is evidenced in the increased number of conservancies that have been registered since its inception. There has been an overall increase in the understanding of tourism within local community structures which has led to the refinement of best practices, processes and approaches. It has been noted in the literature that most sustainable tourism programmes fail due to lack of support from either the government or the private sector. In Namibia, the Government has endeavoured to increase its support for conservancies through relevant legislation and policies. The private sector has not disappointed either; investing a lot of money towards tourism development through up-market products and on-going capacity building for locals. Despite these actions, the dynamic nature of the environment renders it susceptible to external factors which have the potential to undermine the principles of sustainable tourism. To continue to develop the conservancy sector in a sustainable manner, there is a need to: attract investment from additional institutions such as the World Bank and the African Development Bank; remove barriers in accessing finance; and address land tenure and marketing issues. Greater investment in this sector would enable the development of necessary infrastructure, employment and skills, and would help to overcome the challenges of marketing CBTs. Furthermore, policy interventions are needed regarding local communities' full participation in CBTs that enable communities to take control of joint venture enterprises when a JV contract expires.

■ Summary and Conclusion

The case study has reviewed complex issues linked to community based tourism development in Namibia. The promulgation of an inclusive tourism policy document has enabled the Namibian Government to pursue tourism as a development strategy. Coupled with assistance from the international donor community and exploiting the abundance of natural resources and diverse communities, tourism has become a source of livelihood for the rural poor. The study has shown that partnerships can prove mutually beneficial, yielding benefits for the rural poor in the form of hunting quotas and revenues from tourist activities, guiding and the selling of crafts and other wares, but that sufficient planning is required to achieve sustainable livelihoods. The case also demonstrates the extent to which government can influence development through tourism while remaining congruent with the conservation efforts of other stakeholders. The theoretical frameworks reviewed help to put the case into context by identifying connections between tourism and rural development. The study further highlights the significance of natural resource preservation, wildlife management and local community empowerment and offers insights into the ways in which the complexity of tourism can be harnessed to concurrently pursue both development and conservation strategies.

11

■ Study Questions

1   Based on the case study, discuss the concept of a communal conservancy in Namibia. Analyse the challenges faced by the Government in addressing socio-economic problems confronted by the rural poor in Namibia. Briefly explain the policies that have helped in the formation a community level conservancy in Namibia

2   Studies have shown that there is a need for partnerships; not exclusively between the private sector and communities, but widely across the industry due to the diversity of stakeholders. To what extent do these partnerships have the potential to result in sustainable tourism development and what measures should be taken to ensure that these partnerships yield tangible results?

3   The future of the community conservancy sector is bright in Namibia. Suggest five major points that should be addressed to ensure that this dream is realised and that the destination capitalises on its competitive advantage.

4   Discuss the challenges faced by CBT and recommend mitigation measures that would ensure the achievement of sustainable tourism development without compromising social equity, environmental sustainability, and economic efficiency.

5   Discuss the major achievements of Community Based Natural Resources Management in Namibia.

■ Useful Sources and Links

Draft Tourism Policy 2001 – 2010, retrieved from http://www.namibweb.com/tourpolicy.htm on 12 August 2012.

Employment and Economic Growth (TIPEEG), retrieved from http://www.npc.gov.na/publications/ TIPEEG.pdf on 01 January, 2013

German International Cooperation (GIZ) 2010/2011. Environmental Law and Policy in Namibia , retrieved from http://www.environment-namibia.net/constitution.html on 05 January 2013

Index Mundi (2013). Namibia - international tourism, retrieved from http://www.indexmundi.com/facts/namibia/international-tourism on 12 August 2012.

MET (2008). *Namibia Tourist Arrivals*, retrieved from http://www.namibia tourism. com. na/trade_cat_sub.php?sub_cat_id=32 on 15 September 2012.

MET (2010) Tourist Statistical Report, retrieved from http://www.namibiatourism.com. na/ research-center/ on 12 August 2012.

MET (n.d.) DRAFT TOURISM POLICY 2001 – 2010, retrieved from http://www.namibweb.com/tourpolicy.htm on 01 January 2013.

NACSO (2009). Living with wildlife -the story of Namibia's Communal Conservancies, retrieved from http://www.nacso.org.na/SOCprofiles/Namibia's%20 Communal% 20 Conservancies.pdf on 01 January 2013.

NACSO (2009). Promotion of Community Based Tourism Policy Document Number 9. June 1995, Ministry of Environment and Tourism, retrieved from http://www.nacso. org.na/dwnlds/MET_policy_on_CBT_development.pdf on 01 January 2013

NACSO (2010). Conservation and the Environment in Namibia - 2010 / 2011, retrieved from http://www.venturepublications.com.na/ezines/conservation_10_11/index. html on 01 January 2013

Namibia Tourism (2013). Namibia tourism Research Center, retrieved from http:// www.namibiatourism.com.na/research-center/ on 12 August 2012.

Namibian (2012). Twenty years of booming tourism, retrieved from http://www. namibian.com.na/index.php?id=28&tx_ttnews%5Btt_news%5D=65894&no_cache=1 on 12 August 2012.

NATIONAL PLANNING COMMISSION (2011). Targeted Intervention Program for

The National Planning Commission (n.d). National Development Plan, retrieved from http://www.npc.gov.na/npc/ndp3info.html on 01 January 2013.

The National Planning Commission. Vision 2030, retrieved from http://www.npc.gov. na/ vision/vision_2030bgd.htm on 01 January 2013.

WTTC (2008). Progress and priorities 2008/09, retrieved from www.wttc.travel on 12 August 2012.

WTTC (2009). *NAMIBIA*, retrieved from http://www.wttc.org/eng/Tourism_Research/ Tourism_Impact_Data_and_ForecastTool/ on 15 July 2012.

■ References

Ashley, C. (1999) *Joint Venture Contracts. Contractual Issues for Communities and their Tourism Partners. Guidelines for Practitioners*, Harare: Africa Resources Trust

Ashley, C. (2000) *The Impacts of Tourism on Rural Livelihoods: Namibia's Experience.* Chameleon Press: London

Barnes, I.J., MacGregor, J. and Weaver C.L. (2001) 'Economic analysis of community wildlife use initiatives in Namibia', retrieved from http://www.dea.met.gov.na On 10 October 2012.

Barnes, I.J., MacGregor, J. and Weaver C.L. (2002) 'Economic Efficiency and Incentives for Change within Namibia's Community Wildlife Use Initiatives', *World Development,* **30** (4), 667–681.

Faulkner, B. & Tideswell, C. (1997) 'A framework for monitoring community impacts of tourism', *Journal of Sustainable Tourism*, 5 (1), 3-28.

Gächter, S. & Fehr, E. (1999) 'Collective action as a social exchange', *Journal of Economic Behaviour & Organisation*, **39**, 341–369.

11

Giaoutzi, M. & Nijkamp, P. (2006) *Tourism and regional development: new pathways*, Aldershot: Ashgate Publishing Ltd.

Government of the Republic of Namibia (1990) *The Constitution of the Republic of Namibia*. Windhoek: Government.

Government of Namibia (1996) 'National Conservation Amendment Act', *Government Gazette of the Republic of Namibia*, Windhoek, Namibia.

Hoole, A. and Berkes, F. (2010) 'Breaking down fences: Recoupling social–ecological systems for biodiversity conservation in Namibia', *Geoforum*, **41**, 304–317.

Jones, B.T.B. (1995) "Wildlife Management, Utilization and Tourism in Communal Areas: Benefits to Communities and Improved Resource Management", DEA Research Discussion Paper, No 5, Directorate of Environment Affairs, Ministry of Environment and Tourism, Windhoek, Namibia.

Jones, B.T.B. & Luipert, S. (2002) 'Best Practices for the CBNRM Programme to work with Regional and Local Authorities, Traditional Authorities and line ministries to facilitate Integrated and Collaborative support to Community-Based CBOs working on Common-Property Natural Resource Management', A Consultancy Report to the Namibian Association of Community-Based Natural Resource Management Support Organisations (NACSO).

Jones, B.T.B. & Murphree, M. (2004) 'Community-Based Natural Resource Management as a Conservation Mechanism: Lessons and Directions', in B. Child (ed.) *Parks in Transition: Biodiversity, Rural Development and the Bottom Line*. Earthscan: London.

Jones, BTB. (2003) 'Selected Natural Resource Management & Limited Rural Development Assessment', Study Carried out for USAID/Namibia Strategy for 2004-2010.

Jones, S. (2005) 'Community-based ecotourism: The significance of social capital', *Annals of Tourism Research*, **32** (2), 303-324.

Long, S.A. & Jones, B.T.B. (2004) 'Contextualising CBNRM in Namibia', in A.S. Long (ed.) *Livelihoods and CBNRM in Namibia. The Findings of the WILD Project*, Windhoek: Ministry of Environment and Tourism.

Long, S.A. (2004) (Ed.) 'Livelihoods and CBNRM in Namibia: The Findings of the WILD Project', Final technical report of the Wildlife Integration for Livelihood Diversification Project (WILD), prepared for the Directorate of Environmental Affairs and Parks and Wildlife Management, The Ministry of Environment and Tourism, The Government of the Republic of Namibia, Windhoek.

Matose, F. (2004) 'Breaking New Ground' *A Conceptual Framework for Research on People-Centred Approaches to Natural Resource Management in Southern Africa*. A CASS/PLAAS Research and Communications Programme Concept note, retrieved from: www.cassplaas.org on 15 October 2012.

McGehee, N.G. & Santos, C. (2005) 'Social change, discourse and volunteer tourism', *Annals of Tourism Research*, 32 (3), 760–779.

McIntosh, A. J. & Zahra, A. (2007) 'A cultural encounter through volunteer tourism: Towards the ideals of sustainable tourism?', *Journal of Sustainable Tourism*, **15** (5), 541–557.

MET (2010) *Sharing Best Practices for Integrated Sustainable Land Management in the Drylands of Southern Africa: The Practicalities*. Windhoek, Namibia.

MET (2008) *Policy on Tourism and Wildlife Concessions on State Land*, Windhoek, Republic of Namibia: Ministry of Environment and Tourism.

MET (2002) 'Namibia's Natural Resource Sector. A Contribution to Vision 2030. Special Case Study. Conservancies and Community-Based Natural Resource Management (CBNRM) Initiatives in Namibia and their Contribution to Poverty Alleviation in Rural Areas', retrieved from http://www.sasusg.net/ on 10 October 2012.

Midgley, J., Hall, A., Hardiman, M. and Narine, D. (1996) *Community Participation, Social Development and the State*, Suffolk: Richard Clay Ltd.

Murphree, M. (2004) 'Communal Approaches to Natural Resource Management in Africa: from whence and to where?', Keynote Address to the 2004 Breslauer Graduate Student Symposium. California: Berkeley.

Murphy, C. & Roe, D. (2004) 'Livelihoods and Tourism in Communal Area Conservancies', in A.S. Long (ed.) *Livelihoods and CBNRM in Namibia. The Findings of the WILD Project*, Windhoek: Ministry of Environment and Tourism.

Murphy, E.P. & Murphy, E.A. (2004) *Strategic management for Tourism Communities: Bridging the Gaps*, Clevedon: Channel View publications.

NACSO (2010) *Namibia's Communal Conservancies: a Review of Progress* 2010, Windhoek, Namibia: NACSO..

Ndlovu, J., Nyakunu, E. & Auala, A. (2011) 'Community Based Tourism in Twyfelfontein Conservancy: Exploring Local Community's Involvement', *International Journal of Hospitality and Tourism Systems*, **4** (2), 38-46.

Pretty, J. (2003) 'Social capital and the collective management of resources', *Science*, **302** (5652), 1912-1914.

Purdue, R.R., Long, P.T. and Allen, L. (1990) 'Resident support for tourism development', *Annals of Tourism Research*, **17** (4), 586-99.

Ribot, J.C. (2004) *Waiting for Democracy: The Politics of Choice in Natural Resource Decentralization*, Washington, DC: World Resources Institute.

Sebele, S.L. (2010) 'Community-based tourism ventures, benefits and challenges: Khama Rhino Sanctuary Trust, Central District, Botswana', *Tourism Management*, **31**, 136–146.

Shackleton, S., Campbell, B., Wollenberg, E. and Edmunds, D. (2002) 'Devolution and community-based natural resource management: creating space for local people to participate and benefit?', *ODI Natural Resource perspectives*, Number 76, March 2002.

Sharpley, R. & Telfer, J.D. (2002) *Tourism Development: Concepts and Issues*, Clevedon: Channel View.

11

Tacconi, L. (2007) 'Decentralization, forests and livelihoods: Theory and narrative', retrieved from www.sciencedirect.com on 15 October 2012.

Trick, P. (2000) *Policy Framework for Community-Based Natural Resources Management in Malawi: A Review of Laws, Policies & Practice*. Blantyre: Community Partnerships for Sustainable Resource Management in Malawi.

12 Whale Watch Kaikoura

Stephen L. Wearing, *University of Technology Sydney*

Paul A. Cunningham, *Rikkyo University*

Synopsis and Learning Outcomes

Leading up to 2001, the international whale-watching industry was valued at over US$1 billion (Hoyt, 2001), and attracted over 9 million people annually. According to the International Fund for Animal Welfare (IFAW), by 2008 the number grew to over 13 million people, participating in over 119 countries and its economic value is estimated to be worth in excess of US$2.1 billion per annum in revenue (O'Connor *et al.*, 2009:8). The WWK venture is one of the first whale-watching companies in this rapidly globalising field.

Internationally, the annual growth rate for whale watching exceeds that of tourism. The growth rate in five of the seven regions in of the world: Asia (17% per year), Central America and the Caribbean (13% per year), South America (10% per year), Oceania and the Pacific Islands (10% per year) and Europe (7%), provides evidence of the strength of this emerging industry (O'Connor *et al.*, 2009). Based on this trajectory of growth, the IFAW suggests that whaling countries would benefit from switching to whale watching. Whale watching has become a valuable resource for tourism and the destination communities that are able to develop it. Kaikoura, located on New Zealand's South Island, is one example of a community which has developed this activity and whose reputation as a whale-watching destination is growing.

Whale Watch Kaikoura (WWK) is New Zealand's only marine-based whale-watching company, operating year round and offering visitors an exciting and up-close encounter with sperm whales. WWK is an indigenous, 100% Maori owned and operated venture in the small coastal town of Kaikoura. The company has played a vital role in rebuilding the local economy through the development of community-based tourism in Kaikoura. The company was founded in 1987 by local Maori to create jobs for local Maori and to establish an economic base for the Ngati Kuri community. It has since grown into a multi-million dollar ecotourism business. WWK has been successful in developing a business run by the local, indigenous community while at the same time meeting the requirements and guidelines of ecotourism, including those related to whale watching. The profitability of WWK has enabled them to secure the Kaikoura Peninsula, which has been occupied by Maori for about 1,000 years and which was at risk of being lost to overseas investors.

Many community-based ecotourism operators are working within a new politico-economic space, created by the shared language of 'sustainability' and a more mainstream environmental agenda. Many of these groups are keenly aware of the relationships between environmental issues and tourism that have come into prominence, especially the interrelationships between humans and environmental risks. This chapter examines the WWK from this perspective.

After completing this case study learners should be able to understand:

1   The way local ecotourism ventures can meet the varying demands of sustainability, in respect of how this term is conceived, applied and implemented into the management of such enterprises.

2   The scope and scale of the economic, social, cultural and biophysical impacts of whale watching as a tourism activity in a variety of contexts.

3   The relationship between whaling, whale-watching tourism and the natural environment.

4   The policies and industry-based initiatives related to whale watching as a sustainable tourism activity.

■   Background

WWK is located in the small coastal town of Kaikoura, a two and a half hour drive northeast of Christchurch, on New Zealand's South Island (see Figure 12.1 and Figure 12.2). Kaikoura is widely known as one of the leading ecotourism destinations in New Zealand, and WWK has driven community development through interactive wildlife activities focusing on the natural environment. WWK specialises in providing guests with an exciting, up-close encounter with the world's largest toothed predator — the giant sperm whale — in its natural environment. Whale-watching tours take place all year round (weather permitting).

Whale Watch was established in 1987, at a time when Maori were suffering from a decline in the Kaikoura economy. Kati Kuri leaders believed that the local sperm whales held the answer to unemployment in the local the Maori community. This view was grounded in belief that their ancestor 'Paikea' had journeyed to a new life in New Zealand on the back of the whale 'Tohora'. It therefore seemed appropriate for Paikea's descendants to once again ride on the back of the whale in search of a new life.

The Kati Kuri founders of Whale Watch mortgaged their houses in order to secure a loan to start the business. In the early days, small inflatable boats were used. Over time, these were replaced by a larger boat with an upper viewing deck — the 'Uruao'. Today, the Whale Watch fleet includes four modern catamarans especially designed for whale watching. The expansion of the Whale Watch fleet resulted in the building of a new marina in South Bay. It is from here that all whale watching tours currently depart (source: http://www.whalewatch.co.nz/content/who-we-are).

Figure 12.1: Locating WWK. Source: http://www.kaikoura.co.nz

WWK is a 100% Maori-owned business with two indigenous shareholders. Governance is provided by a Board of Directors and the Chief Operating Officer, the company's senior executive, who reports directly to the Chairman of the Board (see Organisational Chart). The COO and his management team oversee all the day-to-day operations and functions of the company. WWK hires up to 50 full-time employees and as many as 75 employees during the peak season (e.g. cleaners, guides, captains, maintenance, customer service, retail & merchandise, food & beverage, transport, administration, marketing, communications, management), making the company one of the largest employers in the region. Other large employers in Kaikoura include Fonterra, New World Supermarket, Kaikoura Mill, and EDI Works.

12

Figure 12.2: Kaikoura Peninsula. Source: http://www.kaikoura.co.nz

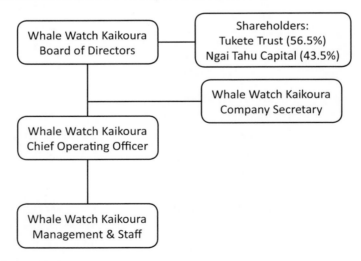

Figure 12.3: Organisational Chart

WWK has established itself as a benchmark of ecotourism and sustainable development. WWK has also played a major role in the transition of Kaikoura, which has evolved from a rest stop to a tourism destination in its own right. The success of WWK has also led to the development of other tourism related activities, accommodation, restaurants, cafes and retail outlets in the local area. WWK envisions its future as the destination, experience and company of choice. It endeavours to identify, develop and promote 'wow-based' experiences. The company values customers, community, conservation and culture.

WWK's strategic goals include:

- To promote Kaikoura as a holiday destination that results in sustainable growth and development.
- To position the company as the top nature-based tourism operation in New Zealand.
- To financially empower the company to achieve its *wawata* (dreams and aspirations).
- To earn customers' admiration and advocacy.

WKK currently has more than 100,000 visitors per annum. Its customer base is comprised of 80% international and 20% domestic visitors. International visitors are comprised of 60% European (UK, Germany, etc.), 15% North America (USA, Canada), 10% Australia, 10% Asia, and 5% other (South America, Pacific Islands, etc.). In recent years there has been a notable increase in visitors from the Asian market, led by China.

Figure 12.4: One of the Whale Watch vessels. Source: http://www.kaikoura.co.nz

WWK has developed into one of New Zealand's leading tourism operations and iconic experiences. WWK has won numerous awards for its efforts, such as the 2011 PATA Gold Award in Environment & Eco-tourism, the 2010 WTTC Tourism for Tomorrow Community Benefit Award, and the 2009 Supreme Winner Virgin Holidays Responsible Tourism Award. WWK is also a New Zealand Qualmark Endorsed Visitor Activity and is New Zealand Qualmark Enviro Award Gold Accredited.

This case study explains how organisations like WWK provide an example of the way in which a local indigenous community can move away from the cultural debate on whaling (cf. Orams, 2001) and consider how whale watching might provide alternative means of economic sustainability for these communities. In a study focusing on marine ecotourism as a potential agent for sustainable development, Orams (2002:338) found that in the case of Kaikoura, New Zealand, the tourism industry has helped transform the town from being economically depressed to becoming one of New Zealand's boomtowns by providing local employment opportunities and through the development of ecotourism activities and growth potential of this industry.

■ Key Concepts

In 2001, the *Journal of Sustainable Tourism* published an article looking at the transition from whale hunting in Tonga to whale watching (Orams, 2001). Since then the overnight growth of the whale-watching industry has 'industrialised the ocean' (Corkeron, 2004:848). Viewed by the International Whaling Commission (IWC) in 1983 as an alternative 'use' for whales, today whale-watching is recognised as a legitimate form of **ecotourism** (Orams, 2000) and viewed by some as 'an acceptable form of benign exploitation' (Gillespie 2003:408). This case study is presented within the framework of ecotourism, looking at its value for the **community** that established it and the visitors who participate in this activity.

Whale watching falls within the realm of ecotourism. It focuses on the aesthetic and visual consumption of whales, while at the same time emphasising the educative component of this activity. Some types of whale watching are more tactile, notably programs that offer the chance to swim with dolphins. Whether viewing whales from a promontory point on land or from the bow of a boat, this activity fosters use and appreciation of these creatures that is sustainable in nature.

Ecotourism has created a market value for the observation of animals through the **commodification** of wildlife and its habitats. However, the commodification and consumption of animals through whaling and whale watching has been criticised by some on ethical grounds (Scarpaci *et al.*, 2008), especially the commercial harvesting of these creatures. Ecotourism sits between the absolutes of conservation and commercialisation, where the consumptive human 'gaze' of wildlife is central to the experience (Ryan & Saward, 2004:246). Given its alignment to alternative tourism (Wearing & Neil, 2009), ecotourism should also provide a mechanism to improve animal welfare and to conserve nature in general. Since whale watching is widely considered to be a bona fide ecotourism activity, its strong environmental protection objectives may lead to positive imaging of animal welfare and attract more whale-watching tourists (Kuo *et al.*, 2009:6).

Ecotourism is an extension of the sustainability discourse and a model of tourism development that embraces the preservation of ecology and culture. According to the Japan Ecotourism Society (JES, 2010), ecotourism should utilise unique local natural, historical and cultural resources; promote the conservation and preservation of local resources through appropriate management; and activate local communities through responsible tourism and economic development that makes sustainable use of the natural and social resources. Ecotourism Australia (EA, 2010) defines ecotourism as ecologically sustainable tourism with a primary focus on experiencing natural areas that fosters environmental and cultural understanding, appreciation and conservation. Whale watching has proven to be a sustainable practice. Worldwide, "the whale watching industry has grown at an average rate of 3.7% per year, comparing well against global tourism growth of 4.2% per year over the same period" (O'Connor *et al.*, 2009:23).

By scrutinising the intersection of globalised and localised environmentalism in Lajes do Pico (Azores, Portugal) at the historical juncture when whale watching superseded whale hunting in this village, Neves-Graça (2006) sheds light on cultural valuations for these marine resources and how they evolve through interaction. Neves-Graça explains how localised environmentalism (including the ecological knowledge and practices of local inhabitants) was reproduced, learned, and transformed within the context of globalised environmental concerns (Ibid:19). Conversely, globalised, macro-cultural discourses have an influence upon local actors — interweaving local and distant dialogs into a mutually constituted, albeit contested, narrative.

Incorporating a comprehensive model of ecotourism that adopts a holistic and global approach to attractions such as whale watching and interpretation can foster environmental enhancement, deep understanding, and the transformation of behaviour (Weaver, 2005). Weaver argues that this model can best promote global sustainability by accommodating selective 'hard' and 'soft' characteristics, thereby taking advantage of the economies of scale offered by the latter (Ibid:439).

12

Promoting whale watching through the model of ecotourism acts upon the local and global discourses on conservation, the intersection of which would mark the cutting edge of this narrative, and provides a way forward. In spite of the contested nature of use versus conservation — this discourse would appear to be moving in favour of the latter, particularly given the current concern about global warming and other environmental issues. The promotion of whale watching provides the opportunity to pursue the fastest growing segment of ecotourism — and tourism in general, and at the same time demonstrates commitment to the preservation and conservation of natural resources at the local level. The case of WWK provides an example of how this can be done in a way that meets all these intentions.

■   Case Analysis

Patrick Ramage, the Director of the IFAW whale program, notes that whale watching revenues have more than doubled since 1998, and that whale-watching operations around the world now include 3,330 operators and employ an estimated 13,200 people, with the fastest growth seen in Asia (O'Connor *et al.*, 2009). Ramage adds, "While governments continue to debate the future of whaling, the bottom line is increasingly clear: Responsible whale watching is the most sustainable, environmentally-friendly and economically beneficial 'use' of whales in the 21st century" (O'Connor *et al.*, 2009: 9).

One of the central tenets of ecotourism is education, which is fundamentally important to conservation and other environmental action. Whale watching encourages people to appreciate and protect whales through their interaction and participatory experience with these creatures. Encounters with wildlife have been shown to create a need within people to help protect them (Lien, 2001), and has the potential to promote the development of conservation through the long-term effects of attitudinal changes towards wild animals and natural habitats (Duffus & Dearden, 1993).

Whale watching also provides the opportunity to educate people about other environmental issues affecting our oceans and waterways — such as high toxin levels and pollution, and can act as a platform from which commercial tour operators can educate their tourists about long-term sustainable benefits of whale-watching. WWK have invested significant time and capital in developing interpretive narration aboard their vessels, which runs for the duration of the experience, aimed at imparting new information to the tourist on the marine wildlife they encounter and their conservation. WWK believes the experience shows the tourist the significant value of whale watching as opposed to whale hunting.

Various factors qualify WWK as a special case: close-up observation of whales, including rare sperm whales, and the use of environmentally-friendly operated vessels. The success of WWK has played a major role in transforming the local community. It has driven economic development, provided employment for local

Maori and other community members, advocated for the conservation and protection of whales and has become a well-known, international whale-watching destination.

WWK not only operates a profitable business, but also provides direct and indirect employment for the local community. Furthermore, it provides other tangible community benefits by offering complimentary annual whale-watching school trips; by providing donations to Kaikoura St John Ambulance, the coastguard and fire brigade; and by funding various marine research projects – to name a few.

However, the growth of whale watching in Kaikoura has not gone uncontested. The development of a successful ecotourism business run by indigenous Maori caused some resentment early on among a small minority of residents who found it difficult to accept the Maori success and who were misinformed about the development of whale watching in Kaikoura. This led to the firebombing of a bus, the sabotaging of a number of vessels. Threats were made to individuals in the company but these matters have since been resolved (pers. com. Kauahi Ngapora, WWK, 2013)

In the future, issues related to the impacts of whale-watching tours on marine mammals will be of significant interest. Martinez and Orams (2011:191) note that few studies have focused on quantifying sound produced by tour boats while viewing marine mammals, or by the deliberate use of sound to create and enhance interactions between tourists and targeted species. The authors argue that an alternative approach to management is needed in order to minimise any potential harm to the animals.

The latest research carried out in Kaikoura over a three-year period, *Effects of Tourism on the Behaviour of Sperm Whales inhabiting the Kaikoura Canyon 2011* has not shown any increased pressure on whales at this location (Markowitz et al., 2011). The researchers used a passive directional hydrophone to locate whales in Kaikoura by listening to their sonar and did not emit any noise to create or enhance interactions with marine mammals. The research above undertook studies of noise made by tourist vessels, namely those of WWK, and found that the jet propulsion systems adopted for use in their fleet are very quiet particularly when manoeuvring around the whales.

This case study provides an example of how indigenous peoples and the special relationship they have with the land and nature, and their long-established practices of sustainable development can be beneficial. Sofield (2002:118) posits that embracing ecotourism is a good 'sociological fit', and provides a means to revitalise that "interdependency and extend the human-biosphere relationship" in new directions.

12

This indigenous stewardship is evident in this case study and provides support for the widely held belief in the ecotourism literature that such involvement and commitment is necessary. However Fennell (2008:129) questions the legitimacy of ecological stewardship as an innate characteristic of traditional societies, and suggests that traditional societies found it difficult to manage resources in a sustainable way. This suggests that others besides the indigenous Maori might be qualified to work in the management and conservation of whales as a natural resource and as indispensable actors in the activity of whale-watching.

Furthermore, few case studies have devoted attention to community-based ecotourism management from the perspective of indigenous governance and decision-making systems. To this end, Farrelly (2011: 817) provides a methodology that considers the core Fijian concept of 'vanua' (way of life), involving "inter-related social, ecological and spiritual elements." An emic perspective that makes use of informal 'talanoa' (discussion) is used and examined, along with the roles of "kin groups, village spokesmen and clan systems, and their relationship with western business decision-making practices." Such research helps to elucidate the value of indigenous versus non-indigenous stewardship within the context of community-based management of whale watching.

■ Future Outlook

The case of WWK shows how a local community has moved beyond the contested debate on the relative merits of whaling versus whale watching by adopting the latter as a sustainable resource. The WWK has embraced whale watching as both an emerging cultural and economically sustainable product and, in turn, whale watching has served the community well. This case study demonstrates how whale watching as an ecotourism activity with appropriate organisational structures and regulation has the capacity to take a leading role in the development of a community based ecotourism industry (cf. Hoyt 2005: 141).

WWK presents itself as a case in point, whereby the model of ecotourism has been embraced and underpins the activity of whale watching at this location. By definition, this involves the local community and creates a sense of ownership and common purpose. This acts to validate the value and use of whales in a credible and sustainable way — and promotes other sustainable development in the form of construction, retail development and so on.

The Last Word – Success at a Local Level

Indigenous Maori-owned and locally operated, WWK has won the Community Benefit Award for its outstanding achievement in rebuilding the local economy through community-based tourism in Kaikoura, which is located on the east coast of South Island in New Zealand. WWK specialises in giving more than 100,000 annual visitors the opportunity for up close observation of marine life, including rare sperm whales, using environmentally-friendly operated vessels. The company was founded in 1987 by local Maori to create jobs for the indigenous Ngati Kuri community, and has since grown into a multi-million dollar nature tourism business. Kauahi Ngapora, the COO of WWK, notes:

Whale Watch is committed to carefully managing its use of a rare natural resource. We will cherish this award, just as we cherish our values of hospitality to visitors and reverence for the natural world. (http://www.wtmwrtd.com/files/whale_watch_kaikoura_ltd.pdf)

■ Summary and Conclusion

Whale and dolphin watching has now become the fastest growing sector of the ecotourism industry (Corkeron, 2004; Curtin, 2003). Although whale watching is part of the global tourism trade, it is really a community level industry. Whale-watching tourists support local economies through their purchases, from whale-watching tickets to associated expenses for travel, lodging, food, and souvenirs. This supports local businesses, creating jobs and providing income (O'Connor *et al.*, 2009). In addition to growing the local economy, the whale-watching industry offers communities a sense of identity and cultural pride and helps foster an appreciation for the marine environment, upon which whose resources provide the foundation for growth.

There are many advantages of this kind of ecotourism. If conducted responsibly, this activity is relatively benign (Blewitt, 2008; Jensen *et al.*, 2009; Lusseau *et al.*, 2009; Noren *et al.*, 2009). Through proper management, whale watching has proven to be both profitable and sustainable. This approach provides a resource for ongoing cetacean research as well as a context in which to promote an appreciation of the marine environment and to explore conservation issues in the public discourse (Greenpeace, 2010).

Whale watching has widely been viewed as a harmless activity with considerable educational and conservation benefits. However, as a cautionary note there is growing concern about the incidental stress caused to the animals during the activity of whale watching. The questions scientists, policy makers and tourism industry leaders are facing are how to determine the conditions under which

12

whale watching becomes detrimental to the animals it targets, and how to best protect them (Simmonds & Isaac, 2007). Higham and Lusseau (2007, 2008) have echoed the urgent need for empirical research into whaling and whale watching. Whale Watch Kaikoura appear to have found solutions to many of the concerns raised and research is supporting their approach (cf. Markowitz *et al.*, 2011).

There is little doubt that ecotourism operations such as WWK has contributed to the commodification of wildlife worldwide and has at the same time created a market value for the viewing of nature. As a result ecotourism is becoming more valuable to small coastal communities by creating, via tourism, an economic value for the ecotourism outputs. The whale has always had a commercial value and with the growth of whale watching, it now sits between the absolutes of economic consumption and visual consumption, where the direct human 'gaze' of wildlife is central to the experience, with all of the possibilities for disruption that such viewing brings (Ryan & Saward, 2004:246). Its growing popularity and alignment to alternative tourism (c.f. Wearing & Neil, 2009) provides an opportunity to promote understanding and awareness of whales across diverse populations of whale watchers, while at the same time providing a sustainable livelihood for local communities.

WWK provides a vehicle for developing the local economy through ecotourism within the context of conservation. Given the political nature of the environment (e.g. Latour, 1993) and the way in which it is consumed, local communities can address this issue at a local level, dealing with whaling and whale watching from both political and cultural perspectives. The discourse on promoting whale watching over whaling has to be addressed within the context of the beliefs, attitudes and values of the local communities that are engaging in or seeking to engage in it. Lawrence and Phillips (2004) explored this question in a case study that examined the development of commercial whale watching on the western coast of Canada. Lawrence and Phillips argue that the emergence of this activity was made possible through the influence of the macro-cultural discourse upon local actors in the creation of new institutional structures, i.e. commercial whale watching companies – and their profitability. The changing conceptualisation of the whale in North America, along with the "geographically distinct institutional fields" that emerged depended on local action and the process of "structuration that those actions supported" (p. 689).

Communities and organisations such as WWK can help to develop a global code of ethics that will help to regulate the growing whale watching industry over time. By adopting the model of ecotourism, with its built-in code of ethics, it would provide a vehicle to pursue and promote whale watching as a socially and economically sustainable activity — while at the same time adhering to the general principles of conservation. Ecotourism provides a model for development that has proven to be an engine for economic growth and the development of political capital. Aligning whale watching with ecotourism allows it to be repositioned as a dynamic socio-cultural activity that is economically vibrant.

WWK has demonstrated that the conceptual shift from hunting whales to whale watching acts to localise the dialogue of conservation and nature management. Whale watching management encompasses a macro, meso and micro dialog that contributes to the way we view whales on the local and global levels.

■ Study Questions

1 Discuss how a community-based tourism organisation such as WWK is acting sustainably. Provide reasons and examples to support your answer.

2 What evidence does Orams (2001) provide for the case under study? Give reasons and examples to support your answer.

3 In the debate on whaling versus whale watching, should cultural rights be prioritised over animal rights within the context of sustainable tourism? Give reasons and examples to support your answer.

4 Read Lawrence and Phillips (2004) and outline the discourse that led to an evolution from whaling to whale watching at this location. Is the main reason for this change related to an economic return or are there other factors?

5 Provide an outline of sustainable practice that can be used in whale watching to ensure that it does not impact on the whales.

■ References

AFP (2009) 'Whales worth more alive than dead, says new report', *Sydney Morning Herald,* 24 June, retrieved from http://news.smh.com.au/breaking-news-world/whales-worth-more-alive-than-dead-says-new-report-20090624-cvjd.html on 5 April 2010.

Amante-Helweg, V. (1996) 'Ecotourist's beliefs and knowledge about dolphins and the development of cetacean ecotourism', *Aquatic Mammals,* **22** (2), 131-140.

Anderson, G.R.V., Forbes, M.A. & Pirzl, R.M. (1996) 'A national overview of the development of whale watching in Australia', in S. Cogan, S. Presser & A. Jeffery (Eds.) *Encounters with Whales - 1995 Proceedings,* Canberra, Australia: Australian Nature Conservation Agency, (pp. 5-16).

Black, R. (2009) 'Whale-watching 'worth billions', *BBC News Online,* retrieved from http://news.bbc.co.uk/2/hi/sci/tech/8114353.stm on 8 April 2010.

Blewitt, M. (2008) 'Dolphin - human interactions in Australian waters', *Australian Zoologist,* **34** (SPEC. ISS.), 197-210.

12

Boo, E. (1990) *Ecotourism: The Potentials and Pitfalls (vols 1&2)*. Washington, DC: WorldWide Fund for Nature.

Brydon, A. (2006) 'The Predicament of Nature: Keiko the Whale and The Cultural Politics of Whaling in Iceland', *Anthropological Quarterly, 79* (2), 225-260.

Clark, J., Simmonds, M. & Williams-Grey, V. (2007) 'Close encounters: Whale watching in the UK', *Biologist, **54**, (3), 134-141.

Cloke, P. & Perkins, H.C. (2005) 'Cetacean performance and tourism in Kaikoura, New Zealand', *Environment and Planning D: Society and Space, **23** (6), 903-924.

Cole, S. (2007) 'Implementing and Evaluating a Code of Conduct for Visitors', *Tourism Management, **28** (2), 9.

Corkeron, P.J. (1996) 'Research Priorities for whale watching in Australia: a scientist's viewpoint', in: K. Cogan, S. Presser & A. Jeffery (Eds) *Encounters with Whales - 1995 Proceedings*, Canberra, Australia: Australian Nature Conservation Agency, (pp. 123-135).

Corkeron, P. J. (2004) 'Whale watching, iconography and marine conservation', *Conservation Biology*, 18, (3), 847-849.

Corkeron, P. (2006) 'How shall we watch whales?', in D. M. Lavigne (Ed.) *Gaining Ground: In Pursuit of Ecological Sustainability*, Guelph, Canada: International Fund for Animal Welfare, (pp. 161-170).

Cunningham, P.A. (2002) 'Attitudes towards ecotourism in the Ogasawara islands among lodging owners on Chichijima', *Tokyo Toritsu Daigaku Ogasawara Kenkyu Inkai [Nenpou]*,27, 1-29.

Cunningham, P.A. (2007) 'Baselining Sustainable Practices in Ogasawara', *Rikkyo Daigaku Kankogakubu Kiyo, **9**, 44-49.

Curtin, S. (2003) 'Whale-watching in Kaikoura: Sustainable destination development?', *Journal of Ecotourism, **2** (3), 173-195.

Denardo, C., Dougherty, M., Hastie, G., Leaper, R., Wilson, B. & Thompson, P.M. (2001) 'A new technique to measure spatial relationships within groups of free ranging coastal cetaceans', *Journal of Applied Ecology, **38**, 888-895.

Duffus, D.A. & Deaden, P. (1993) 'Recreational use, valuation and management of Killer Whales (*Orcinus orca*) on Canada's Pacific coast', *Environmental Conservation, **20** (2), 149-156.

Ecotourism Australia (2010) 'Ecotourism Australia', Australia, retrieved from http://www.ecotourism.gr.jp/ on 5 June 2010.

Einarsson, N. (2009) 'From good to eat to good to watch: Whale watching, adaptation and change in Icelandic fishing communities', *Polar Research, **28** (1), 129-138.

Farrelly, T. A. (2011). 'Indigenous and democratic decision-making: issues from community-based ecotourism in the Boumā National Heritage Park, Fiji', *Journal of Sustainable Tourism, **19** (7), 817-835.

Fennell, D.A. (2008) 'Ecotourism and the myth of indigenous stewardship', *Journal of Sustainable Tourism, **16** (2), 129-149.

Foxlee, J. (2001) 'Whale watching at Hervey Bay', *Parks and Leisure Australia*, **4** (3), 17–18.

Free Willy-Keiko Foundation (2010) Free Willey Keiko Foundation, Berkeley, USA, retrieved from http://www.keiko.com/index.html on 8 April 2010.

Gillespie, A. (2003) 'Legitimating a whale ethic', *Environmental Ethics,* **25**, (4), 395-410.

Graci, S. (2010) 'The potential for aboriginal ecotourism in Ontario', *Geography Research Forum*, **30**, 135-148.

Greenpeace (2010) Iceland whaling, Greenpeace, Australia, retrieved from http://archive.greenpeace.org/whales/iceland/WhaleWatching.htm on 26 April 2010.

Herrera, G.E. & Hoagland, P. (2006) 'Commercial whaling, tourism, and boycotts: An economic perspective', *Marine Policy,* **30** (3), 261-269.

Higham, J.E.S. & Lusseau, D. (2007) 'Urgent need for empirical research into whaling and whale watching', *Conservation Biology,* **21** (2), 554-558.

Higham, J.E.S. & Lusseau, D. (2008) 'Slaughtering the goose that lays the golden egg: Are whaling and whale-watching mutually exclusive?', *Current Issues in Tourism,* **11** (1), 63-74.

Higham, J.E.S., Bejder, L. & Lusseau, D. (2008) 'An integrated and adaptive management model to address the long-term sustainability of tourist interactions with cetaceans', *Environmental Conservation,* **35** (4), 294-302.

Hobson, K. & Essex, S. (2001) 'Sustainable tourism: A view from accommodation businesses', *The Service Industries Journal,* **21** (4), 133–146.

Hoyt, E. (1996) 'Whale watching: a global overview of the industry's rapid growth and some implications and suggestions for Australia', in K. Cogan, S. Presser & A. Jeffery (Eds,) *Encounters with Whales - 1995 Proceedings*, , Canberra, Australia: Australian Nature Conservation Agency, (pp. 31-36).

Hoyt, E. (2001) *Whale Watching (2001) Worldwide Tourism Numbers, Expenditures, and Expanding Socioeconomic Benefits*, London: International Fund for Animal Welfare.

Hoyt, E. & Hvenegaard, G.T. (2002) 'A review of whale watching and whaling with applications for the Caribbean', *Coastal Management*, **30** (4), 381-399.

Hoyt, E. (2005) 'Sustainable ecotourism on Atlantic islands, with special reference to whale watching, marine protected areas and sanctuaries for cetaceans', *Biology and Environment*, **105** (3), 141-154.

International Foundation for Animal Welfare (IFAW) (2010) 'The Booming Whale Watching Industry', International Foundation for Animal Welfare, Australia, retrieved from http://www.mywhaleweb.com/?page_id=289 on 6 April 2010.

International Whaling Commission (IWC) (2006) Taiji Declaration on Traditional Whaling. Submission by Japan, IWC/58/11, Agenda item 10, International Whaling Commission.

Japan Ecotourism Society (2010) Japan Ecotourism Society, Tokyo, Japan, retrieved from http://www.ecotourism.gr.jp/on 5 June 2010.

12

Jensen, F. H., Bejder, L., Wahlberg, M., Soto, N. A., Johnson, M., & Madsen, P.T. (2009) 'Vessel noise effects on delphinid communication', *Marine Ecology Progress Series*, **395**, 161-175.

Khatchadourian, R. (2010) 'Street fight on the high seas', *The New Yorker*, retrieved from http://www.newyorker.com/online/blogs/newsdesk/2010/2001/sea-shepherd.html on 2 July, 2010.

King, D.A. & Stewart, W.P. (1996) 'Ecotourism and Commodification: Protecting People and Places', *Biodiversity and Conservation*, **5**, 13.

Kirk, D. (1996) *Environmental Management for Hotels*. Oxford: Butterworth.

Kuo, H., Chen, C.C., & McAleer, M. (2009) 'Estimating the Impact of Whaling on Global Whale Watching', unpublished paper, retrieved from http://ssrn.com/abstract=1442444 on August 1 2010.

Latour, B. (1993) *We Have Never Been Modern*, Cambridge, MA: Harvard University Press.

Lawrence, T.B. & Phillips, N. (2004) 'From Moby Dick to Free Willy: Macro-cultural discourse and institutional entrepreneurship in emerging institutional fields', *Organisation*, **11** (5), 689-711.

Leaper, R. & Gordon, J. (2001) 'Application of photogrammetric methods for locating and tracking cetacean movements at sea', *Journal of Cetacean Research and Management*, **3** (2), 131-141.

Lien, J. (2001) 'The Conservation Basis for the Regulation of Whale Watching in Canada by the Department of Fisheries and Oceans: A Precautionary Approach', Canadian Technical Report of Fisheries and Aquatic Sciences 2363, Toronto, Canada.

Lück, M. (2003) 'Education on marine mammal tours as agent for conservation - But do tourists want to be educated?', *Ocean and Coastal Management*, **46** (9-10), 943-956.

Lussean, D. (2004) 'The hidden cost of tourism: Detecting long-term effects of tourism using behavioral information', *Ecology and Society*, **9** (1), 2.

Lusseau, D., Bain, D.E., Williams, R. & Smith, J.C. (2009) 'Vessel traffic disrupts the foraging behavior of southern resident killer whales Orcinus orca', *Endangered Species Research*, **6** (3), 211-221.

Macnaghten, P. & Urry, J. (1998) *Contested Natures*, London: Sage Publications.

Mainichi Daily News (2010) 'Australia's legal action against Japan over whaling retrieved from as pre-election move', 2 June, retrieved from http://mdn.mainichi.jp/mdnnews/news/20100602p2a00m0na012000c.html on 3 June 2010.

Markowitz, T.M., Richter, C. & Gordon, J. (2011) 'Effects of Tourism on the behaviour of Sperm Whales inhabiting the Kaikoura Canyon', Submitted to the New Zealand Department of Conservation by PACE-NZRP: Kaikoura Sperm Whales and Tourism Research Project. New Zealand.

Martinez, E. & Orams, M.B. (2011) 'Kia angi puku to hoe I te wai: Ocean noise and tourism', *Tourism in Marine Environments*, **7** (3-4), 191-202.

Masutani, M. (2010) 'No solution in sight for fight over whales', *The Japan Times*, 26 January, retrieved from http://search.japantimes.co.jp/cgi-bin/nn20100126i1.html on 2 July 2010.

Mori, K. (2000) 'An example of ecotourism in Ogasawara Islands-Actualities and problems of whale watching', Kagoshima International Conference on World Natural Heritage, May 18 – 21.

Muloin, S. (1998) 'Wildlife tourism: the psychological benefits of whale watching', *Pacific Tourism Review*, **2**, 199-213.

Neil, D.T. & Breeze, L. (1998) 'Topics of interest to participants in human-marine mammal interactions: a preliminary report', in M.B. Roams & D.T. Neil (Eds.) *Dolphin and Whale Research at Tangalooma 1989-1998*, Auckland, NZ: Massey, (pp. 167-171).

Neves-Graça, K. (2004) 'Revisiting the tragedy of the commons: Ecological dilemmas of whale watching in the Azores', *Human Organisation*, **63** (3), 289-300.

Neves-Graça, K. (2006) 'Politics of Environmentalism and Ecological Knowledge at the Intersection of Local and Global Processes', *Journal of Ecological Anthropology*, **10**, 19-32

Noren, D.P., Johnson, A.H., Rehder, D. & Larson, A. (2009) 'Close approaches by vessels elicit surface active behaviors by southern resident killer whales', *Endangered Species Research*, **8** (3), 179-192.

O'Connor, S., Campbell, R., Cortez, H. & Knowles, T. (2009) 'Whale Watching Worldwide: tourism numbers, expenditures and expanding economic benefits', a special report from the International Fund for Animal Welfare, prepared by Economists at Large, Yarmouth MA, USA.

Ohmagari, K. (2002) 'Whaling conflict and Japan: Whale as eco-political resource', in T. Akimichi & N. Kishigami (Eds) *Dispute of Ocean, Kyoto: Jimbun-shoin*, (pp. 246–250).

Orams, M.B. (2002) 'Marine ecotourism as a potential agent for sustainable development in Kaikoura, New Zealand', *International Journal of Sustainable Development*, **5**(3), 338-352.

Orams, M.B. (2001) 'From whale hunting to whale watching in Tonga: A sustainable future?', *Journal of Sustainable Tourism*, **9** (2), 128-146.

Orams, M.B. (2000) 'Tourists getting close to whales, is it what whale-watching is all about?', *Tourism Management*, **21** (6), 561- 569.

Orams, M.B. (1995) 'Development and management of a feeding program for wild bottlenose dolphins at Tangalooma, Australia', *Aquatic Mammals*, **21** (2), 137–147.

Parsons, E.C.M. & Draheim, M. (2009) 'A reason not to support whaling - a tourism impact case study from the Dominican Republic', *Current Issues in Tourism*, **12** (4), 397-403.

Parsons, E.C.M., Lück, M. & Lewandowski, J.K. (2006) 'Recent advances in whale-watching research: 2005-2006', *Tourism in Marine Environments*, **3** (2), 179-189.

12

Parsons, E.C.M., Warburton, C.A., Woods-Ballard, A., Hughes, A. & Johnston, P. (2003) 'The value of conserving whales: The impacts of cetacean-related tourism on the economy of rural West Scotland', *Aquatic Conservation: Marine and Freshwater Ecosystems*, **13** (5), 397-415.

Randburg.com (2010) 'Whales around Iceland', Randburg, Iceland, retrieved from http://randburg.com/is/whales-around-iceland/index.asp on 10 April 2010.

Ota, K. (2007) 'Whalemeat in Japanese school lunches found toxic'. *Reuters*, August 1, retrieved from http://www.reuters.com/article/idUST6359120070801 on 2 July 2010.

Ryan, C. & Saward, J. (2004) 'The zoo as ecotourism attraction - Visitor reactions, perceptions and management implications: The case of Hamilton Zoo, New Zealand', *Journal of Sustainable Tourism*, **12** (3), 245-266.

Scarpaci, C., Parsons, E.C.M. & Lück , M. (2008) 'Recent advances in whale-watching research: 2006-2007', *Tourism in Marine Environments*, **5** (1), 55-66.

Segi, S. (2003) SPC Traditional Marine Resource Management and Knowledge Information Bulletin #15 – July.

Simmonds, M.P. & Isaac, S.J. (2007) 'The impacts of climate change on marine mammals: Early signs of significant problems', *ORYX*, **41** (1), 19-26.

Sofield, T.H.B. (2002) 'Australian aboriginal ecotourism in the wet tropics rainforest of Queensland, Australia'. *Mountain Research and Development*, **22** (2), 118-122.

Sousa-Lima, R.S. & Clark, C.W. (2008) 'Modeling the effect of boat traffic on the fluctuation of humpback whale singing activity in the Abrolhos National Marine Park, Brazil', *Canadian Acoustics - Acoustique Canadienne*, **36** (1), 174-181.

Stamation, K. (2008) 'Understanding human-whale interactions: A multidisciplinary approach', *Australian Zoologist*, **34** (SPEC. ISS.), 211-224.

Stamation, K.A., Croft, D.B., Shaughnessy, P.D., Waples, K.A. & Briggs, S.V. (2007) 'Educational and conservation value of whale watching', *Tourism in Marine Environments*, **4** (1), 41-55.

Stamation, K.A., Croft, D.B., Shaughnessy, P.D., Waples, K.A. & Briggs, S.V. (2010) 'Behavioral responses of humpback whales (*Megaptera novaeangliae*) to whale-watching vessels on the southeastern coast of Australia', *Marine Mammal Science*, **26** (1), 98-122.

Takahara, K. (2007) 'Whaling — for nationalism or science?' *The Japan Times Online*. 25 December, 2007, retrieved from http://search.japantimes.co.jp/cgi-bin/nn20071225i1.html on 8 April 2010.

Tisdell, C. & Wilson, C. (2005) 'Perceived impacts of ecotourism on environmental learning and conservation: Turtle watching as a case study', *Environment, Development and Sustainability*, **7** (3), 291-302.

Tosi, C.H. & Ferreira, R.G. (2009) 'Behavior of estuarine dolphin, Sotalia guianensis (Cetacea, Delphinidae), in controlled boat traffic situation at southern coast of Rio Grande do Norte, Brazil', *Biodiversity and Conservation*, **18** (1), 67-78.

Valentine, P.S., Birtles, A., Curnock, M., Arnold, P. & Dunstan, A. (2004) 'Getting closer to whales - Passenger expectations and experiences, and the management of swim with dwarf minke whale interactions in the Great Barrier Reef', *Tourism Management,* **25** (6), 647-655.

Vieira, N. & Brito, C. (2009) 'Past and recent sperm whales sightings in the Azores based on catches and whale watching information', *Journal of the Marine Biological Association of the United Kingdom,* **89** (5), 1067-1070.

Wearing, S.L. and Neil, J. (2009) *Ecotourism: Impacts, Potential and Possibilities,* 2nd Edition, Oxford: Butterworth-Heinemann.

Weaver, D.B. (2005) 'Comprehensive and minimalist dimensions of ecotourism', *Annals of Tourism Research,* **32** (2), 439-455.

Weinrich, M.T., & Corbelli, C. (2009) 'Does whale watching in Southern New England impact humpback whale (Megaptera novaeangliae) calf production or calf survival?', *Biological Conservation,* **142**, 2931–2940.

Whale and Dolphin Watch Australia (2010) Whale & Dolphin Watch, Australia, retrieved from http://www.whaleanddolphinwatchaustralia.com.au/research.php on 8 April 2010.

Wight, P. (1993) 'Ecotourism: Ethics or Eco –Sell', *Journal of Travel Research,* **31** (3), 11.

Wight, P. (1994) 'Environmentally responsible marketing of tourism', in E. Cater & G. Lowman (Eds.) , *Ecotoursim: A Sustainable Option?,* New York: Wiley.

Wildlife Extra (2009) 'An end to Japanese whaling? Massive cuts to subsidy may force an end to Japanese whaling', retrieved from http://www.wildlifeextra.com/go/news/japanese-whaling931.html on 8 April 2010.

Wiley, D.N., Moller, J.C. & Carlson, C. (2004) 'Compliance with voluntary speed guidelines by the commercial whale watching industry in and around the Stellwagen Bank National Marine Sanctuary', Paper SC/56/WW9 presented to the IWC Scientific Committee, Sorrento, Italy.

Williams, R., Bain, D.E., Smith, J.C. & Lusseau, D. (2009) 'Effects of vessel on behaviour patterns of individual southern resident killer whales orcinus orca', *Endangered Species Research,* **6** (3), 199-209.

Williams, R. & Crosbie, K. (2007) 'Antarctic whales and Antarctic tourism' *Tourism in Marine Environments,* **4** (2-3), 195-202.

Woods-Ballard, A.J., Parsons, E.C.M., Hughes, A.J., Velander, K.A., Ladle, R.J. & Warburton, C.A. (2003) 'The sustainability of whale watching in Scotland', *Journal of Sustainable Tourism,* **11** (1), 40-55.

Zeppel, H. & Muloin, S. (2008) 'Conservation Benefits of Interpretation on Marine Wildlife Tours', *Human Dimensions of Wildlife: An International Journal,* **13** (4), 280 – 294.

12

Index